TAMING THE COMPENSATION MONSTER

Using Freight Broker Compensation to Drive Urgency, Performance, and Profits

Beth Carroll

INDIE BOOKS
INTERNATIONAL

ISBN-10: 1-941870-74-0
ISBN-13: 978-1-941870-74-7
Library of Congress Control Number: 2016956031

Designed by Joni McPherson, mcphersongraphics.com

INDIE BOOKS INTERNATIONAL, LLC
2424 VISTA WAY, SUITE 316
OCEANSIDE, CA 92054
www.indiebooksintl.com

Table of Contents

SECTION I

The Monster Problem for Freight Brokers

Chapter 1

What's Wrong with Traditional Freight Broker Compensation?

Freight brokers are companies that act as intermediaries in the moving of freight throughout the United States. They agree to move freight for a shipper for a fee and then find a carrier who will move the freight for an amount that is less than the fee the shipper is paying the broker (hopefully). You can think of this as buying capacity from a trucking company at a low price, then adding value-added services to that capacity and selling it to a shipper at a higher price. Brokers collect money from shippers (revenue) and pay money to carriers (purchased transportation) and retain the difference (margin/profit) to run their businesses. Generally, a broker owns no assets (trucks) but may be connected to an asset provider, or they may own a few assets. The roles used as examples in this book are those found at typical non-asset, spot-market brokerage organizations. Companies that provide asset-based services or full transportation management services, such as full LTL (Less Than Truckload) shipping management, TMS (transportation management system) services, and freight bill auditing, will certainly find the material herein valuable, but some adaptation will be needed to apply these concepts to those types of roles.

Many of the original brokers used a cradle-to-grave organizational model (one person managed all aspects of the buying and selling of capacity) and often were paid using a 100 percent variable, straight-commission model. So, what's wrong with this approach for paying your employees?

Nothing wrong at all. That is, if every employee has the same opportunity, the same skills, the same training, and all your freight is from the spot market, where each day is a new day and no one knows for sure what's coming his or her way.

However, as this industry has matured, many freight brokers have found the traditional approach no longer works for them. This is especially true in organizations with substantial business from contracted or long-standing "house" accounts, or those moving toward more sophisticated organizational structures (such as using strategic account managers, strengthening the use of outside selling roles, and/or splitting the organization between teams of "freight finders" and "truck finders," who may or may not be tied together in shared dependency).

Identifying the Compensation Beast

The compensation beast can rear its ugly head in many ways. But generally, compensation problems for freight brokers come from what I call the "four employee lacks":

- Lack of urgency
- Lack of motivation
- Lack of good decision-making
- Lack of alignment with company objectives

The purpose of this book is to provide better compensation information for transportation and logistics providers to help them create a sense of urgency, inspire motivation, promote better decision-making, and give rewards that align with company objectives.

The challenge many brokers face when managing their compensation arrangements is to accomplish these objectives within a system that is "fair." If you use a highly variable plan delivered via a flat commission rate, is it fair to pay an employee the standard commission rate for moving freight for a large contracted account they didn't land? What about for freight that is generated by an outside salesperson—shouldn't there be a reduced rate on these loads? What if you are using a team approach that generates a shared pool, but now you need to add people to the team? Or you need to move your best team leader to another group that is substantially smaller because you know he or she will be able to grow it?

In each case, if you stay wedded to using a highly variable commission-only approach, you will find yourself creating "special deals" in which certain accounts are paid a lower (or higher) rate than others, in which you are administering cumbersome calculations to deduct the "lead generation" fee before calculating the commission, or in which you are creating temporary "deals" with employees as you reorganize your staff or your accounts. You may find yourself spending more time trying to remember the different compensation arrangements you have for Joe, Sally, and Fred, and what the rates are for accounts A, B, and C, than you spend building relationships with your customers.

Using the traditional, highly variable, straight-commission approach for incentive compensation is appealing on many levels: it's simple, easy to understand, it's economically "pure" so you don't have to worry that you're going to spend all your profits on incentives, and it's easy to administer (at least at first). For busy business leaders, this approach feels like it should be a "fix-it-and-forget-it" solution. In addition to these benefits, the commission mechanic (regardless of how much pay is at risk in the plan) is a powerful tool that creates an intensity of focus you generally don't find with other compensation mechanics.

For these reasons, using a highly variable pay plan, with a commission mechanic to calculate pay, is perfectly appropriate for some selling roles and in some selling situations, especially for pure new-business-hunters in start-up companies or high-growth divisions of established companies. These types of roles have what is called "high prominence," which means, in plain language, that they have a high degree of control over the outcome of their sales efforts. (I would still suggest using an escalating or de-escalating commission mechanic even for these roles, however, as it's rarely appropriate or advisable to base an entire incentive plan on a single, unchanging commission rate.)

Where the traditional highly variable commission-based approach does not make sense, however, is for companies that have developed a substantial book of regular business, are building strong brand awareness in the marketplace, or are using multiple internal resources to land and grow accounts. In these cases, most of the employees are "less prominent" in the sales process; they are a cog in a much larger wheel that includes marketing and advertising campaigns, outside sales resources, and long-standing company relationships with customers.

Using the traditional approach can hinder management from making the right changes for their business (shifting customers or load volume around) because it would be "taking pay" away from one employee and "giving it" to another. In these circumstances, the better approach is to shift your pay mix more toward base salary (at least 50/50) and to make at least part of the incentive plan dependent upon attaining defined goals.

What is a Goal-Based Incentive Mechanic (aka "Bonus")?

Commissions pay for volume ("the more you sell, the more you make"). Goal-based bonuses pay for attaining a predefined goal ("if you beat your goal, you make more money"). Using goal-based incentive mechanics can provide more flexibility for managers to run their business to meet customer needs, target strategic objectives beyond gross profit, and manage employee pay as a motivational tool.

An example might help illustrate the difference.

Joe, who has been given a large volume of mainly long-standing accounts, generates $30,000 in profit in this month. This is down 25 percent from what he did the last month.

Sally, who is still developing her book of accounts, generates $15,000 this month, which represents 150 percent growth over what she did the last month.

A pure-commission mechanic would pay Joe twice as much as Sally, even though his business is shrinking and hers is growing. Arguably, Sally is doing a better job than Joe, even though (and I can hear many of you saying it) "Joe is still bringing more money into the company." Yes, he is. But, once a company grows beyond the point of living hand-to-mouth in start-up mode, management needs to think strategically in terms of what behaviors and results should be rewarded for the long-term growth of the company. Sally could very well be a better long-term asset, but she may not stay around too much longer if her pay is below market-competitive levels (and also very likely perceived by her as being "not fair" compared to what "that slouch, Joe" is making).

Using a pure goal-based mechanic, Joe might be given a monthly goal of $35,000 per month in profit, and Sally a goal of $12,500. Management would make this determination based on previous-period performance, opportunities for growth, and the overall numbers that must be hit by the organization. At 100 percent of goal, each would make $1,000 for the month. A well-designed goal-based plan has a range around goal (called a performance range) which allows for payout both below and above goal, with different escalation rates. At $30,000, Joe would be at 85 percent ($30,000/$35,000) of his goal, and he might be paid 77.5 percent of his target incentive, or $775. At $15,000, Sally would be at 120 percent ($15,000/$12,500) of her goal, and she might be paid 140 percent of her target incentive, or $1,400. This provides a payout that is determined by the individual's ability to meet and exceed the goal that management has set for him/her. Next month, when management decides that Sally might do a better job managing one of Joe's accounts, Joe's goal would be reduced and Sally's would be increased to reflect this shift in accounts. Each of their incentive targets would still be $1,000 for 100 percent of goal attainment. Management can make this decision purely based on what is in the best interests of the customer and the company, without fear that this kind of change is taking pay from Joe and "giving it" to Sally. Instead, the discussion is entirely about who is best suited to manage and grow this particular account.

For those of you who may feel that the pure goal-based approach is not quite right for your business, or it's too much change to take in one step, there is the comforting fact that there are hundreds of different ways to design incentive plans. One of these options is to use a goal-based commission mechanic in which the commission rate increases when the individual's goal is attained. This provides a blend of reward for volume and reward for goal-attainment. Another option is to divide the incentive into two (or three) elements, one of which is paid using a commission mechanic, and the other of which is paid using a goal-based mechanic. Some companies elect to transition by using the goal-based mechanic on a lesser-weighted team measure, leaving the commission mechanic on a more heavily weighted individual measure. The possibilities are truly endless, and by moving beyond the traditional broker method for compensating their employees, many companies are finding answers to some of their most vexing compensation problems.

Chapter 2

Top Six Compensation Mistakes

What are the ways the compensation beast will bite you? Let me count the ways.

I am often asked, "what is 'the right way' to pay?" But there is no easy answer to this question. The "right way" depends on a variety of factors particular to each company. But there are some definite wrong ways to pay, and this chapter will outline the six most common compensation mistakes I've seen in my work with hundreds of companies in a variety of industries ranging in size from small, privately-held companies to multi-billion-dollar global giants.

MISTAKE #1: Not Realizing That Compensation Is Part of a Complex and Interconnected System

There are two variations of this mistake. In the first, managers fail to understand that compensation both supports and reflects a company's unique objectives, strategy, structure, and culture. When leaders want me to just "tell them the answer," or "tell them how XYZ broker pays," or when they think they can "just use the plan from their last company," they are making this mistake.

In order to develop the "right" plan for your company, you are going to have to do some work—there is no easy answer. Here are just some of the questions you need to answer *before you even begin to think about a commission rate*:

- Define your business objectives and strategy:
  - What are your specific financial goals for the next year and the next five years?
  - How are you going to succeed? What has worked in the past? What has not?
  - What is your competitive advantage? Do you offer a low-cost solution or a high-service solution? Do you have a technological advantage or a relationship advantage?
  - What do your clients think of you? What do you want them to think?
  - Are you focused on short-term growth or long-term stability?
  - Are you positioning for acquisition, developing a legacy, or do you need to think about a future change in control?
- Define the optimal organization structure and roles for your organization:

- What is the right business flow?

- How much interdependency exists (or should exist) between people, roles, groups, and divisions?

- What risks come from different structures (**TIP:** Some organizational structures make it easier for employees to leave and/or start their own brokerage than others).

- What structures will allow for clear and focused incentive plans? (**TIP:** If you have more than ten people and every person has a different incentive plan, or everyone has the same incentive plan, you don't have role clarity and need to do more work in this area—chapter 3 can provide some guidance.)

- Define your organization's optimal culture:

  - Do you want a culture of competition, of cooperation, or someplace in between?

  - How much control does management need or want to have over the way things are done?

  - How much variation in pay is optimal for your culture?

  - How paternalistic is the company?

  - Does your organization allow people to take risks and learn from their mistakes, or are there many rules that control choices?

  - Does the organization promote a higher purpose than simply making money? (**TIP:** None of your employees are going to be enthusiastic about work if they know the only reason they are working is so you can buy your next luxury car or your next vacation home.)

- Define your competitive position in the labor market:

  - What do current and potential employees think about the organization? What do you want them to think?

  - What benefits do you offer?

  - Is the company well-regarded, or does it have some reputational issues?

  - How well-trained and regarded are the managers?

  - Is there a good training program for the employees and opportunity for continuous learning?

  - Is the environment high-spirited and fun, somber, relaxed, or professional?

  - Does the company use a performance management system allowing for salary increases? When was the last time you gave raises?

– How are successes celebrated? How are failures managed?

– What career advancement opportunities exist?

(**TIP:** if your company scores high on many of these questions, then you may be able to pay a bit below market rates in your cash compensation plan; if you score low then you will literally need to overcompensate.)

The answers to these questions will provide a picture of your company that is unlike any other, and your compensation plans should reflect and support your unique strengths and help to overcome any weaknesses you identified. Chapter 3 will give you more insights into helping you define your goals, and chapter 19 will ensure you use these goals when testing the economics of your new compensation plans.

The second variation of this mistake is to develop compensation plans for highly interconnected roles separately from one another. I am often asked for a plan for sales, or for carrier coordinators, or for account managers because that may be a particular pain point at the moment. It is likely, however, that a change to the incentive plan for any one of these roles will have a ripple effect on the other roles. It's not easy, but the right way to develop new incentive plans is to consider *all* of the roles in your organization at once so you can be sure the plans encourage people to work together and not against each other.

Also, it is essential to do the economic modeling for the full system at once to be sure the total cost of compensation lands in the right range for where your company is in the life cycle and the type of freight you have. (**TIP:** 33 percent is often cited as the "right" cost of compensation as a percent of gross profit, but it is not the only answer, nor is it the right answer for all companies; companies with a large volume of contract or EDI (*electronic data interchange*) freight could be much lower than this, while start-ups, small companies or companies dealing in over-dimensional, heavy-haul or other "high-touch" or specialized freight could be higher and still be perfectly healthy.) Chapter 19 goes into detail on what you can learn through economic modeling that will help you fine tune your compensation plans for maximum return-on-investment (ROI).

MISTAKE #2: Thinking about Compensation as Only an Economic Deal with the Employees

Compensation is about more than money, and those who think about only the math are missing at least half of the point. I tell clients that using an incentive plan is like putting a megaphone on your business strategy. Whatever is in the incentive plan will get a disproportionate amount of attention from employees, so isn't it sensible to spend some time thinking about the message being sent? The plan shouts to employees the company's priorities, ethics, team philosophy, how valuable they are (or aren't) to management, and how many opportunities they have for growth and advancement. Getting the psychology of incentives right is at least as important as getting the math right.

Another mistake in this category is to think about incentive compensation only from the perspective of "how much can I afford to pay." In the sales compensation world, this is called a "cost-of-sales" philosophy. As organizations mature and cash flow becomes less of a concern, management recognizes that knowing the market value of a job is important to attract and retain the type of talent they want. This is called a "cost-of-labor" philosophy and is used by all sophisticated companies once they reach a certain maturity and size. It is at this point that compensation surveys become very important as companies look to the market to understand what is required to pay a competitive wage (and what isn't). Chapter 6 will give you more insights into the proper use of compensation surveys. In some cases, companies will find they are overpaying the market due to legacy issues from the plans they put in place during their start-up phase (see Mistake #3). Developing an understanding of what other companies are paying for the same roles can give management the confidence needed to make adjustments.

Another economic mistake is to think that if a little incentive is a good thing, then a lot of incentive must be better. It is rare that paying 100 percent variable pay to employees (e.g., 100-percent commission plan) is a good thing. Employers lose almost all control when an employee has no salary. The employees may engage in practices that are detrimental to the company's business, customers, carriers, and ethics. The employees are also more likely to jump ship with "their" customers (excuse me, whose customers?) and go for a better offer or start up their own brokerage based on the training, marketing, and technological support *you* gave them.[1]

While a bit of hunger can be a good thing to drive performance, desperation is rarely an effective motivational tool for the long term. If you want your employees to act like used car salespeople, or to run your business the way subprime mortgage brokers ran theirs, then by all means, use a 100-percent variable approach. (**TIP:** AIG and Lehman Brothers were big success stories once upon a time and everyone wanted to know their secrets (see Mistake #1). One of those secrets was a highly variable and highly leveraged incentive plan that rewarded excessive risk-taking and was a proximate cause of the economic collapse of 2008.) If you want an organization with more class than a used car dealership and less risk than a subprime mortgage brokerage, then you will likely need to have some part of your employees' pay coming in the form of a fixed salary. Chapter 4 will give you more insights into the varied psychology behind compensation, and chapter 5 will help you work through the options for selecting the proper pay mix for your different roles.

Companies also get so focused on the economics of compensation that they will spend dollars to save pennies, losing sight of psychological costs and benefits. The best example of this is the development of expensive administrative systems to track adjustments and short

---

[1] I'm aware of the existence of non-compete and non-solicitation agreements that are used widely in this industry. However, they are costly to enforce, create an adversarial relationship with employees, and you are not guaranteed you will win your case.

pays. Provided you have systems in place to prevent egregious errors, there are usually better solutions than holding back, charging back, clawing back, or otherwise demotivating your employees while trying to satisfy some overly heightened sense of fairness and economic precision. (**TIP:** In some states these practices are actually illegal. See Mistake #5.) You are losing hundreds, maybe thousands, of dollars in lost opportunities tracking and arguing over these issues. Would you rather have your employees on the phone getting new customers, or in your accounting department asking to reconcile every load on their last check? Chapter 12 will help you consider options for the appropriate crediting point to optimize the balance between financial risk and employee motivation.

Related to this point, companies often struggle with paying incentives when the company has not hit its profitability goals. This requires a shift in thinking from incentive pay as "profit-sharing" or a "bonus plan" to an integral part of your employees' total compensation package. For incentives to be motivational, they must become part of the expected pay package and employees must be able to predict their pay in advance and be able to affect the outcome through their own efforts. Just as your employees' base salary is not dependent upon your company hitting its EBIT goals, neither should their incentive compensation (except for the highest levels of management). Incentive compensation is a strategic investment made to get results, and if you withhold that pay from your top performers in a down year, then it is likely that your results will be even worse the next year because you will have taught your key people that working hard and getting results doesn't matter.

MISTAKE #3: Not Considering Short-Term and Long-Term Unintended Consequences

Short-term consequences from ill-designed incentive plans typically involve damaging customer and/or carrier relationships and damaging employee interactions. For example, if a plan puts too much pressure on profit percent, you might find your employees negotiating too hard with your customers or carriers and costing the company current business, and worse—the opportunity for future business. Likewise, if a plan rewards only individual performance, then employees may work against each other to maximize their own paychecks. Some familiar examples are carrier reps not letting their colleagues know about available trucks (truck hoarding) or changing the code on a load to their own. I've even heard of reps "paying each other" for loads. If *any* of these things are happening in your office, you have a problem with your incentive plan.

Long-term consequences are harder to anticipate because, by definition, the effects do not manifest themselves for months or even years. The most common long-term consequence is sacrificing long-term growth for short-term gain. This is often found among Branch Managers whose incentive plans pay a percentage of profit. Branch Managers may resist hiring employees under this type of plan, as they will inevitably take a short-term hit in their incentive compensation while they train the new employee. Everyone will agree that in the long run the branch will increase in performance, but managers rarely have the kind of long-term vision as entrepreneurial owners; they are worried about their mortgage and the next car payment. Owners are more willing to take risks than employees, and they are more likely to see the long-term benefit from making "investment" decisions. *Hint: If your employees were willing to take these kinds of risks, they wouldn't be working for you.*

Another long-term consequence is the creation of annuity pay. While it may seem perfectly sensible to arrange a "forever" deal with an outside sales rep who brings new customers (say, 10 percent of all gross profit from that customer for as long as it remains your customer and the rep works for you), five years from now this deal will not make as much sense. For starters, the once-superstar hunter will spend more and more time on nonworking activities (like golf) and your flow of new customers will have dwindled to a trickle. Most importantly, the economics of the deal will no longer make sense because in the intervening years you will have invested in a better Transportation Management Software (TMS) system, a better Customer Relationship Management (CRM) system, support resources, and marketing, all of which make the job *easier* for your sales rep. And yet the sales rep is making the same percentage that he or she made when the job was considerably harder. You must have a system which ensures that your cost of compensation as a percentage of gross profit *decreases* over time, or your business will not thrive. Chapter 15 will give you some alternatives to a straight commission approach that will help you achieve this economic balance.

MISTAKE #4: Not Clarifying Goals to Enable the Shift from Transactional to Growth-Focused Plans

A common complaint from transportation and logistics business owners is the inability to grow. It's no wonder when (1) no one in the organization (including the owner) can articulate a specific growth goal and (2) the compensation plan pays only on a transactional (load-by-load) basis. I say it all the time, but it bears repeating: *"More is not a goal."* You need to make your growth goals clear, to yourself and your employees. There must be accountability when you fail to reach the goals and celebrations when you do. You also need to pay using performance expectations, as this will drive employees to higher levels of performance. At a minimum, you need to use three levels: Threshold, Target, and Excellence.

Threshold is the minimum level of performance required to earn an incentive. If your employees have a base salary, there should be a minimum level of performance before incentives kick in. However, it's rarely a good idea to make this an explicit function of their salary (though I'm well aware many brokers do this, and so do many banks). Effective compensation design actually separates salary and incentives into two different categories of compensation. Salary increases should be earned for teamwork, punctuality, attitude, and any number of other intangibles that differentiate a good employee from a problematic one. Incentives should be used to reward performance in areas that are objective, measurable, relevant to the business, and controllable by the employee. Many brokers miss this opportunity to reward (or correct) the intangibles by never giving salary increases, tying salary increases only to productivity, or by tying incentive thresholds to salary (which actually makes any salary increase feel like a punishment). This is not to say that there should not be an economic relationship between the cost of someone to the organization and their expected productivity—there absolutely *must* be a connection in an aggregated way between the cost of compensation for the employee population and the company's gross profit. But there will be fluctuations in this number over time, and between employees, as some employees provide value that goes beyond pure productivity.

As a good rule of thumb, 90 percent of your employees should be at or above threshold in any pay period, and payout at threshold should be anywhere between 1 percent and 50 percent of the target incentive. If this figure is not being achieved, your incentive plan is not providing much in terms of motivational value.

Target is the level of performance expected from an average performer (sometimes called "quota" or "goal") and should bear some relationship to the growth goals of the organization (the sum of the targets for all employees should equal or slightly exceed the overall company goal). I often refer to a concept called Target Incentive Compensation (TIC). This is the amount of incentive pay earned when target performance is attained. When added to salary, this becomes Target Total Compensation (TTC).[2] When you look at what an employee actually earned in a year (salary plus all cash incentive payments), this is called Actual Total Compensation (ATC) and is the only number that should be compared across companies. Some companies pay more in salary and less in incentive than others. Some companies use a pure-commission approach; others use a commission combined with team incentives, bounties, or other payout mechanics. Comparing just the base salary misses any pay from incentives. Likewise, comparing just the commission rate does not factor in the salary or whether any pay is coming from other components, such as a quarterly team payout. Be wary of companies who report inflated Target Total Compensation figures. A true Target Total Compensation figure should be achievable by 50-60 percent of the employee population. If a company is telling prospective employees (or competitors) that their Target Total Compensation is a figure that has only been achieved by 1 employee in the last five years, they are deceiving themselves, prospects, and the market at large.

Excellence is a bit trickier to define, but a good rule-of-thumb is to look at the top 10 percent of your performers and tie Excellence to the level of productivity they achieve. In Excel, the formula for this is =percentile(*array*,.90) where *array* is the list of performance (such as monthly gross profit) achieved by your employees and .90 represents the 90th percentile, or top 10 percent. (By the way, using =percentile(array,.60) to find the 60th percentile would give you a really good idea of where to set the target productivity level, as this would skew your goals 10 percent higher than the median or 50th percentile actually attained.) Then check to

---

[2] Some compensation consultants refer to this as OTE (On Target Earnings).

see if the sum of targets equals the company goals; if not, then consider how you are going to close the gap (Chapter 20 will give you more advice on how to set and manage goals).

Once you've determined the Excellence level of performance (yes, this is odd grammatically, but it's how compensation consultants talk about it), you then need to determine the appropriate leverage factor. The leverage factor is the multiple of the target incentive earned at Excellence. Typically, it should be 2–3× target, with higher leverage for roles that have more pay at risk. The payout above target should be steeper than it was leading up to 100 percent. This makes sense from the company perspective also, as once an employee has hit target, all fixed costs should be covered and the company can afford to share a higher percent of the profits. See chapter 7 for some additional details on maximizing the motivational value of your plan through the proper selection of mix and leverage.

MISTAKE #5: Not Understanding the Legal Ramifications of Incentive Compensation

Most business owners are (or should be) aware that the misclassification of an employee as exempt from overtime pay can have significant legal and financial ramifications for your company, but some may not be aware that there are also rules that govern incentive compensation as well. For starters, if an employee is nonexempt (paid overtime) and on an incentive plan, then his or her incentive pay needs to be factored into the rate used to calculate his or her overtime pay. Your payroll company should be doing this for you automatically, as this is common knowledge. Of course, for exempt employees who are not paid overtime, this is a nonissue.

Many states also have rules about the handling of certain calculations which are common in commission plans, and you should check with local legal counsel that specialize in labor laws in any state in which your employees work. Of particular concern are "holdbacks" or "chargebacks." Some states frown on the notion that an employee can have "earned" an incentive, but the company is holding that pay pending the completion of some future act (such as payment for a load by a customer). It is far better to simply say that the incentive has not been earned until that act actually happens. Chargebacks can also be problematic, as you are now taking money away that was already paid. Likewise, some states have rules about how and when employees (or agents) may be entitled to pay after they separate from the company. If you think that you are not liable for payments after an employee leaves the company, you may find out the hard way that is not the case if your plan documents have not been worded carefully. (See chapter 22 for additional guidance on documenting your incentive plans.)

At the start of 2013, California legislation Assembly Bill 1396 went into effect, stipulating that any commission plan must be documented and signed by the employee and the manager. California draws a clear distinction between the terms "commission" and "bonus," and it's helpful for employers to do the same to reduce confusion and potentially unnecessary legal scrutiny. "Commission wages are defined as compensation paid to any person for services rendered in the sale of an employer's property or services *and based proportionately upon the amount or value thereof*."[3]

While the world at large tends to use the word *commission* to mean *any variable pay paid to a sales rep*, and *bonus* to mean a *discretionary year-end payout*, compensation consultants use the word *commission* to mean a mathematical formula that determines payout as a percentage of revenue or profit. A *bonus*, or a goal-based incentive, is *a formula that determines a payout based on actual results in relation to a defined goal*. Under a commission plan, someone who sells more makes more. Under a goal-based bonus plan, the person who exceeds his or her goal by the greatest percentage will make the most. For whatever reason, state labor laws scrutinize the structure and rules of goal-based bonus plans less than they do commission plans. Therefore, I recommend using the word *commission* only when it means exactly what state legislatures interpret it to mean (a percent of revenue or profit), and using the term *incentive compensation* when talking about variable pay of any sort. This just helps keep things from getting messy. Why would you want to be scrutinized on your *commission* plan if it's not technically a commission?

MISTAKE #6: Not Communicating and Supporting the Plans, and Not Following Up with Solid Tracking and Feedback

I have saved the worst for last. If you've managed to avoid all of the other mistakes but you still make this one, then you will be no better off than when you started. In fact, you may be worse off because now you will have lost credibility with your staff. When you launch a new incentive plan, you need to back it up. You need to explain it, explain it again, and then explain it again. People have numerous preconceived ideas about incentive compensation based on what they have seen in the past, and they will see any new incentive plan through this lens. It can be very difficult to change this mindset, and you may not realize the points of miscommunication until after you've made the first or second payout under the new plan. It takes two to three pay cycles for employees to truly internalize a new compensation plan. It's only at this point that you will really start to see lasting change in behavior. If you have not reinforced the plan, shown employees performance results, and discussed how they can improve the next time, then you will not get the gains that you need from your plan.

The communication approach to incentive compensation should be as methodical as the design approach. First, you need to be sure your leadership team is onboard with the new design and will support the change. This includes managers and team leaders who will likely be the first line of defense for dealing with complaints (and there *will* be complaints). Bring them into the process early to get their input and buy-in. Then, consider a phased approach for communication.

---

[3] Source: http://www.californiaworkplacelawblog.com/2011/11/articles/legal-articles/california-ab-1396-requires-employers-to-reduce-commission-agreements-to-writing/

Start with a high-level rollout for larger groups of employees. This allows everyone to hear the same thing at once and reduces the amount of "telephone" that is played around the office about the details of the plan. Then set up one-on-one meetings with each employee to give them their goals or performance expectations and explain how they can succeed under the new plan. The focus should be on how they can make more money than they have in the past. They may need to do things differently, but the opportunity for gain should be there. After one-on-one meetings, deliver plan documents that explain how the calculations work in detail and provide examples so the math is crystal clear. Chapter 21 can provide some additional insights to make your communication event a success.

When you write your plan documents, put some thought into how exceptions will be handled. You will not be able to think of everything, but some common points of contention are:

- Vacations or days off: Will employees cover for each other? Will you guarantee a payout?

- New hires: Is there a probationary period or a guaranteed payout during the first few months?

- Terminations: When is the last payment on the incentive plan?

- Transfers: How would you prorate between plans?

- Splitting credit (**TIP:** Avoid it if at all possible.)

- Disciplinary action: If someone is under a performance warning, will they get an incentive?

- Gaming the system (**TIP:** Do not tolerate this at all; terminate immediately.)

Even now, you are not done. You need to provide regular performance reports so employees can monitor their results ahead of their payouts. You will gain nothing if they only find out if they did a good job or a bad job on the day they get their check. They should know ahead of time so they can adjust. The best managers provide constant coaching and feedback and the incentive plan is a perfect excuse to do this. You want them to make as much money as possible, don't you? (You should, if your plan is designed well, because then the company is also making a lot of money. Your interests should be directly aligned with their interests.) By coaching employees and communicating with them about their incentives, you will be working together to maximize their results. They will be happy and your company will see motivated employees driving profitable growth for the company. Chapter 24 will guide you on the things you must do to ensure you get lasting results from your compensation plans.

Now, let's begin our journey as we learn how to tame the compensation beast.

SECTION II

Getting to Know the Nature of Your Beast

Chapter 3

First Step: Define Goals and Roles

PART 1: SETTING GOALS

At the outset of any incentive compensation design project, you must first establish your business goals and put the goals into action. In this chapter, we will look at establishing the baseline (A), setting the goal (B), and doing the analysis to figure out how you will get from A to B. Then we will break down the goals into accountabilities for different roles in your organization and discuss how you might tie these accountabilities to a tightly woven incentive plan framework that aligns each person in each role to the portion of your business plan they can control.

STEP 1: Know Where You are Starting

Begin at the beginning. Spend some time getting to know your business. Freight brokering is a data-rich environment with many statistics available to track and many well-published industry benchmarks. Spend some time looking at your financial reports and your load data to understand your business and how it has changed over time.

There are eleven key statistics (you might call them business KPIs or Key Performance Indicators) to track:

1. Top-line revenue (amount collected from shippers)

2. Purchased transportation costs (amount paid to carriers)

3. Net revenue/gross margin dollars (GM$)/gross profit dollars (GP$) (amount you get to keep to run the business) (#1 minus #2)[4]

4. Margin percent/gross margin percent (GM%)/gross profit percent (GP%) (#3 divided by #1)

5. Load count (or trip, shipment or order count, depending on what is meaningful to your business)

6. Revenue per load (RPL) or revenue per container (RPC) or revenue per shipment (RPS)

7. Profit per load (PPL) or profit per container (PPC) or profit per shipment (PPS)

---

[4] There is no standard industry term for this financial KPI. I have heard it called "Brokerage," "Spread," "Gain," and many other terms. I will call it "Gross Profit (GP)" throughout this book.

8. Cost of compensation for all employees (salary + cash incentives, commissions, bonuses), excluding benefits, employer paid taxes, and owner compensation

9. Cost of compensation as percent of revenue (#8 divided by #1) and percent of gross profit (#8 divided by #3)

10. Net income/operating income (what is left after all expenses are paid)

11. Net income percent (#10 divided by #1)[5]

You will then want to cut these statistics the following ways, looking for trends over time (look at the most recent year versus the prior year, and then look at the quarterly, monthly, weekly, and daily trends):

- Total business

- By customer (how much comes from your top customers?)

- By industry, lane, type of freight or whatever other groupings are significant to your business (look at your customer or lane summary for new groups you may not have noticed before)

- By division, team or unit (this is where looking at cost of compensation as percent of net revenue can be insightful—which groups are generating a better return?)

- By carrier (how concentrated is your carrier base?)

There are good software packages available to help with this analysis. Excel is useful and readily available, but it is limited when you want to do a quick analysis of large volumes of data that you will want to update regularly. It also requires a significant time investment to get really good at it. There is much Excel can do, but most of its true strength remains hidden to casual users, and I've seen companies waste vast quantities of time doing manual analysis in Excel when a small investment in a few training classes could save countless hours and improve their business understanding.

For quicker visualization and more intuitive setup, there are other programs such as Tableau, Good Data and Microsoft BI. Most of these are more expensive than Excel and all will require some training, but it is well worth the effort to be able to see many dimensions of your data at one time. Each year, the main TMS systems offered to this industry add more data-mining and data visualization capability, so be sure you are taking advantage of these add-ons—the insights you will gain are well worth the price.

STEP 2: Establish Long-Term and Short-Term Goals

Once you know where you are starting, define where you want to go. Often companies establish five-year goals and then back into planning the annual growth required to get there. That is fine, as long as the growth expectation is realistic and reflects your staffing plans, the

---

[5] Asset based companies use Operating Ratio (OR) as their key financial metric, which is [(1 - Net Income Percent) x 100]. So a net income percent of 5% is the same as an OR of 95.

economy, and your willingness to work 90 hours a week. As the old saying goes, "If wishes were horses, we'd all ride free," and writing down a goal isn't going to make it happen. It will take hard work and understanding of the different tools at your disposal that will help close the gap from your "as-is" state to your desired "to-be" state. (Some consultants call this "gap analysis." I call it good business planning.)

Step 3: Conduct a Gap Analysis using the RANP Formula

When doing the gap analysis, consultants use another tool called a "PAR analysis." For freight brokers, it should really be called an RANP analysis, as the standard PAR analysis misses one of the key tools that freight brokers have at their disposal: Negotiation. Also, the acronym letters are more logically presented in this order, as it represents the right priority focus.

R = Retention: How much of your business will you retain from the prior year or period? It is rare for the answer to be 100 percent. Look at your history. Understand your customer risks. Establish numbers that represent best-case and worst-case scenarios and use a value in between, but leaning toward the worst-case side.

A = Acquisition: How many new customers can you get in the next year and what will be their average size? Note that you will not acquire all customers on January 1, so you should use the "Rule of 78s" or "Sum of the Digits" to estimate the actual income you will receive in the year from customers acquired throughout the year. The "Rule of 78s" works as follows: if your plan includes acquiring twelve customers at $100,000 in gross profit each, you may be tempted to say this will bring you $1,200,000 in additional gross profit during the year. But this would only happen if all twelve customers started on January 1. If, instead, it is more realistic to think that you will acquire one new customer per month, then you would multiply the total expected revenue by 78/144 (it's around 54 percent) to get a better sense of how much money you will actually collect from these twelve customers during the year.[6]

N = Negotiation: This one you know, or you wouldn't still be in business as a broker, but it's worth spelling out. How much in additional gross profit can you add to the bottom line simply by doing a better job negotiating with carriers? If your top-line revenue was $10,000,000 and you were averaging 14 percent profit, then you kept $1,400,000 in gross profit to run the business. A 1-percent improvement in gross profit percentage means an additional $100,000 in gross profit with no increase in labor costs and no new customers required.

What surprises me is how many brokers know this statistic, even preach this statistic, but then do *nothing* to tie improvement in gross profit percent into the carrier sales incentive

---

[6] If you were to receive the full $100,000 from each customer, you would get twelve months of payments × twelve customers (144 total months of payments). But if you get a new customer each month, then the first customer gives you twelve months, the second gives you eleven months, the third gives you ten months etc. If you add 12+11+10+9...+1, it adds to 78. This is the actual number of monthly payments you will get. This will be 54 percent (78/144) of the full annual total. This percentage works whether you have twelve customers or 300, assuming they are evenly distributed across the months of the year. If it's not an even distribution, add the number of months of revenue you think you will get from each new customer and divide by the total possible months (number of customers × 12) to get your appropriate ratio.

plan. Humans are inherently lazy and will take the path of least resistance. "Should I cover the load now and leave for the day, or try another carrier that I can get a better rate with?" Unless they have a *personal* reason to care, you are incredibly lucky, or extremely good with hiring decisions, most employees will go for the first option. And paying them solely on gross profit dollars (GP$) won't cut it, either, as then you are dealing with the "Bird in the Hand" syndrome—most of the time they will go for the sure thing *now*, even if it means fewer dollars than they could get with a bit more work (and risk). Paying a higher percent commission for a higher gross profit percent (GP%) is a common technique, but often doesn't work quite right either, as employees then swing the other way and do not cover loads they should be covering because they don't want to get paid less. Now you risk losing customers! The answer is often a delicate balancing act between GP$, load count, and GP%, depending on the exact needs of your business (as revealed by conducting the RANP analysis).

P = Penetration: How much more can you get from your existing customers? What low-hanging fruit is being ignored because you don't have anyone specifically focused on growing your existing book of business? What additional lanes or locations could you get from your current customers? Be careful to consider your current customer mix. If you already have a majority of business concentrated in a handful of shippers, your focus needs to be on the R (retention) and the A (acquisition) tools, as you know you are walking a tightrope of risk with too many eggs in too few baskets. Conversely, if you have hundreds of onesie-twosie shippers, then you should probably back off on the A (acquisition) and turn up the heat on the P (penetration).

PART 2: DEFINING ROLES

Next, we will look at how each person in your organization can play a part in helping you close the gap to your goals, and how you can (and should) make it worth their while to do so.

It is common for freight brokers to evolve their organization structure and roles over time, and the typical path is from generalist roles to specialist roles. Understanding these different roles and the appropriate compensation methods to go along with each will help ensure you are getting the most bang for your compensation buck—at each phase in your organization's development.

PHASE 1: "You Eat What You Kill," or "Cradle-to-Grave" Brokering

This is the common one-person-does-all things approach, which I call the "broker" role (note, however, that many people use the term broker when they mean only "carrier sales"—both are fine—just be sure you understand the role being discussed). Under this model, each person in the office is a little office unto themselves. You could set up a profit and loss statement (P&L) on each person, and you might even consider charging a fee if you provide an assistant for support. This approach works for some organizations, but not many, because productivity per person is limited. Very quickly, the person gets swamped with existing business and ceases to call on new customers, or carrier relations get neglected and service failures start to happen.

If you are in the phase where you are still using this role, however, this is the appropriate place for a more traditional percent-of-profit commission plan, and it will likely be highly variable (less from salary, more from incentive) as you are running an office of de-facto agents that you happen to call employees. While it may be simple and easy to structure their commission identically to that of an agent (a fixed split of the profit), this will hinder your ability to grow as your staff's motivation will be limited to their own desired income level. Once they reach the income that meets their needs, most will stop selling. In this model, there is little downside and no leverage. (Leverage is the ability to generate more revenue without proportional effort.) When you add a good administrative resource to your team, and your productivity spikes, that's leverage. Your producers are able to produce more because the routine tasks have been given to someone else, but your costs have not doubled because the administrative resource costs less. The same concept applies to compensation.

Let me explain. In chapter 2, we discussed the concept of a threshold, or point below which no incentive pay is earned. Many of you peg this number to a multiple of the employee's base salary, or to a fixed productivity number based on time in position. What many of you are neglecting, however, is any upside to go along with the downside. Once they've cleared their threshold, the only way they can double their pay is to double their productivity. There is a point where you, as the owner, however, have covered all of your fixed costs and can afford to give a bit more to the employee and in fact, would be happy to do so because every additional dollar beyond this point is dropping straight to your bottom line. It's at this point that you need to add a kicker or escalating commission rate, in order to motivate your staff to get to that higher level of productivity. For example, you may pay them zero percent until they reach their threshold and 5 percent on all profit above threshold. At some higher level of productivity (call it expected performance or target performance) that commission rate could and should increase—possibly to 10 percent or even more. This creates leverage (they can double their pay at less than double the productivity) and creates a "sweet spot" where everyone wants to get to—and where you want them to be, because now it's all "gravy."

One of the tricks here, however, is not to make the rate retroactive. Retroactive commission rates are powerful, but very dangerous because the amount you have to pay out in incentive for $1 in productivity can be huge. Figure 3.1 will illustrate.

Figure 3.1: *Retroactive versus Marginal Commission Structures*

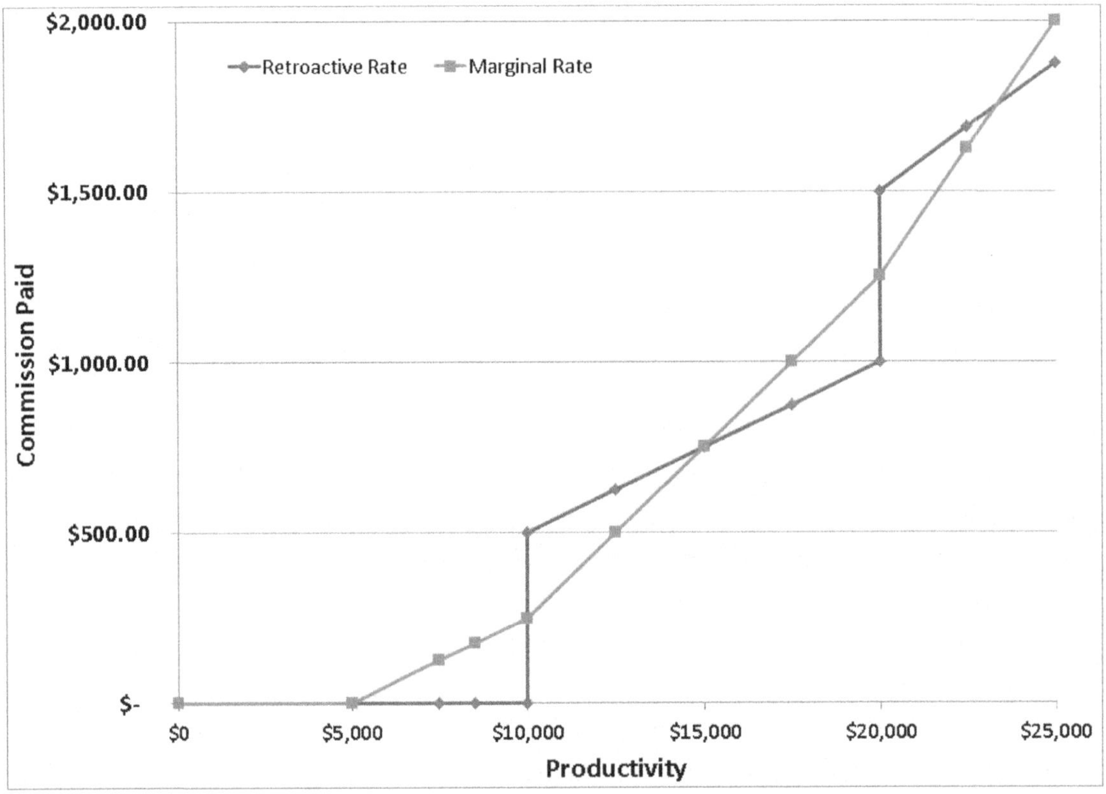

The line with the diamond markers shows a retroactive rate:

- 0 percent paid until $10,000 is reached, then 5 percent paid upon reaching $10,000, retroactive to the first dollar (5 percent × $10,000) = $500

- 5 percent paid on everything until $20,000 is reached, then 7.5 percent paid upon reaching $20,000, retroactive to the first dollar (7.5 percent × $20,000) = $1,500

In this case, the $1 that took the person from $9,999 in productivity to $10,000 was worth $500 in incentive, and the $1 that took them from $19,999 to $20,000 was worth $500. You can see how this is motivational; the employee will do just about anything (including perhaps unethical or dishonest things) to get that $1 additional in productivity. The other problem with a retroactive rate is that people tend to "live" at the top of the incentive step, with limited motivation to get beyond that, particularly if they reach the top of the step close to the end of the month. The additional payout beyond the step bump-up may not be motivational enough to drive them to stay past 4:00 p.m. once they've reached the top of the step.

The line with the square markers shows a marginal rate:

- 5 percent paid on all dollars produced between $5,000 and $10,000 (so the payout at $10,000 is $250, because 5 percent × ($10,000 − $5,000) = $250)

- 10 percent paid on all dollars produced between $10,000 and $20,000 (so the payout at $20,000 is $1,250 because 10 percent × ($20,000 −10,000) = $1,000 + $250 earned at $10,000

- 15 percent paid on all dollars produced above $20,000

While a bit trickier to explain, the marginal commission approach is by far the preferred method among compensation professionals because it smooths earnings while still providing motivational upside—and in fact, can provide GREATER upside to top performers (compare the two lines at $25,000 in productivity).

Without overcomplicating things, a marginal commission approach is likely the most appropriate way to compensate your cradle-to-grave roles, but don't forget to consider adding on strategic elements (such as a new customer bounty) and/or a team-based incentive, as secondary and tertiary components. We will come back again to the concept of retroactive versus marginal commission rates in chapter 15.

PHASE 2: Split Customer and Carrier Sales

The next phase brings the beginning of role specialization and helps improve overall throughput: carrier sales roles are created to focus on the carriers, and customer- or shipper-facing roles are created to focus on the customers (these may be called Account Managers, Account Executives, or Customer Service Reps). Often, at the beginning, they operate as a tightly connected two-person team. Again, this begs for a different compensation approach—one that recognizes the individual efforts of each, and yet rewards them for working together as a team. Also, there would be different approaches for teams that are dealing with existing customers versus teams that are working to find new customers. Over the years, I've seen many variations on this theme, with two-person teams, four-person teams, or teams of customer representatives and teams of carrier sales reps, with no explicit connection between them (the carrier sales reps often are organized regionally by freight origin or destination, whereas the customer reps are usually assigned specific customers). Each structural choice presents its own opportunities and challenges and requires a different incentive approach for each role within the structure.

PHASE 3: Split New and Existing Customers

Once you have a specifically shipper-focused role, you may find you are living a sales force effectiveness truism: when you blend a hunter and a farmer, you get...a farmer. You will find your once-valiant hunters filling up their days with existing customer issues and neglecting to allow time to hunt for new customers. This is not a moral failing on their part—it's simply human nature. Most of us would rather deal with people we know than strangers, and who really enjoys cold-calling and being hung up on repeatedly? So the solution for many companies is to create a separate role whose job is to hunt for new customers exclusively.

They do not retain management duties for these customers once they reach a certain size, but instead hand that duty to a team of account managers who are tasked with nurturing and growing the account even more. It's important to not glorify one of these roles over the other. Both are essential for a healthy company, and both are sales roles. One hunts in the wild, and the other hunts in the zoo. The farmer role should be tasked with growth objectives and new business objectives as well—the source of the new business from farmers will be existing customers, such as sourcing from consignees, or through referrals or discussions with their loyal customer base.

Of course, the compensation arrangements for these two roles must be different, or inequity will rapidly creep into your system because the two jobs are vastly different. A pure-commission approach that only rewards for volume generated does not adequately address that all loads are not created equally—some are easier to get than others. Some are more strategically valuable than others. The existing customer account manager should be paid a higher portion in fixed compensation (salary) than the new business developer, but should have less upside, as successes are less directly tied to their efforts; the customer is already an established business partner. That doesn't mean no upside—just less upside. When your new business developer hits a home run, he should be able to make 3x his target incentive. For an account manager, on the other hand, a home run might mean she earns 2x her target incentive. For an account manager, on the other hand, a home run might mean they earn 2× their target incentive.

The strategic component of the incentive plans will be different as well. You would clearly want some kind of additional reward for a new business developer who lands a premium new customer (tied to your A (Acquisition) goal from step 3) but for your account manager, the strategic objective may be about improved levels of customer service, raising prices, or adding more lanes or locations or types of freight to an existing customer (expanding and deepening the relationship, tied to your P (Penetration) goal from step 3).

PHASE 4: Full-Blown Specialization

The next level of role specialization includes outside sales as well as inside sales to focus on hunting larger accounts with more freight and longer-term contracts. You may also decide to add a carrier development role, whose focus is on building new and deeper carrier relationships. Clearly the incentive plan for these two roles should not be the same because their objectives are different. As you move into the world of longer-term contracts and securing all business in a lane (or even providing full freight management services), you may add inside telemarketer roles as well, whose job is to drum up leads for the outside sales reps, perhaps set appointments, and/or to actually get some new customers among the smaller shipper targets. And you guessed it—this job would have a different incentive plan than all the others: different target total compensation, different pay mix, and different performance measures. For many of the operations roles in this phase of an organization's development, commission-based incentive plans will become problematic and may need to be replaced with goal-based incentive plans.

PHASE 5: Differentiated Sales

Brokerage is evolving to a place that is familiar territory for anyone who has worked with large sales organizations outside this industry—namely, using differentiated outside sales roles. Logistics providers of all shapes and sizes are moving toward customer segmentation: differentiating between strategic customers and transactional customers. This is also sometimes referred to as "contractual" or "strategic" versus "transactional" selling. What the strategic customers require from their salesperson is a different type of relationship. They expect their rep to get to know their business and solve their broader problems, not just offer a quick, cheap, no-frills solution. They are willing to pay more when they can get a more customized, intimate level of service. There will always be transactional customers who just want to purchase on the quick and cheap, and you should not ignore them because this business can fill in holes and create opportunities for future growth. But the type of sales resource you direct to transactional accounts will be vastly different than the person you send after your biggest strategic targets. Needless to say, the pay arrangements for these two selling roles will also be different, with the likely use of management-by-objectives (MBOs)/key performance indicators (KPIs) or milestone bonuses for the "big-game hunters" and a more traditional commission approach for the "small-game hunters."

One of the biggest mistakes I see in this industry is paying an ongoing commission for outside sales. When they land an account (big or small) they should get an incentive for that account for a time, but not forever, and the incentive may not be a commission, but could be a goal-based bonus based on the anticipated twelve-month value of the account. This eliminates the annuity (also called a "phantom base salary") and ensures that your outside sales reps will remain motivated to do what you need them to do—find new customers.

What Should We Call These Roles?

As companies transition to more role specialization, I am often asked for suggested titles for these different roles. Below is a list to get you thinking, based on some of the ones I have seen:

Generic Title and Job Function	Common Titles Used
Carrier Sales (negotiates rates with carriers and convinces them to take a load; may also include some tracking and tracing on the load)	• Carrier Sales Rep (CSR can be a problematic abbreviation as it often stands for "Customer Service" or "Customer Sales Rep") • Logistics Coordinator • Load Coordinator • Operations Rep • Operations Executive • Dispatcher (not recommended due to asset, lack of negotiation connotation) • Broker (not recommended due to ambiguity)
Inside Sales (hunt for new shippers)	• Inside Sales Rep • Sales Rep • Sales Coordinator • New Business Developer • New Business Rep
Account Manager (manage existing shippers, ask for more loads, negotiate spot load rates, enter loads into the system)	• Account Manager • Account Executive • Account Coordinator • Customer Sales or Service Rep (may be a support resource for a higher level role)

Cautions on titles: Your HR department likely has guidelines around the use of the words "manager" and "executive" so be sure to check with them before putting these terms into use in your titles. There is also often an implied hierarchy with the terms "specialist," "analyst," and "coordinator," so be sure you are using them consistently across the entire organization. If "analyst" is the highest-level individual contributor title in your accounting department, then it should also be so in sales and operations. Likewise, managerial titles like "director" and "vice president" should be used in a consistent hierarchical fashion throughout the organization. Chapter 4 will give you more insights into using titles and levels (such as Carrier Sales I, II, and III) to increase motivation from your staff.

Chapter 4

Understanding Compensation Psychology—Increase the Size of Your Toolkit

Now that we have an understanding of where we want to go, how we are going to get there, and what roles we need on the team, it's time for a bit of a discussion about human psychology as it relates to compensation.

In the world of compensation options (and it's a bigger world than most realize), there are two extremes: *100 percent variable pay*, often known as *100 percent commission*, and *100 percent salary*. Neither extreme provides the best motivational bang for the buck, and companies who are using one or the other extreme are missing out on higher levels of motivation, reduced turnover, higher revenue, and lower compensation costs.

Let's tackle the 100-percent-salary model first, as it's pretty easy to see what this is missing. Without incentive pay tied to performance, you are relying on your managers to drive employee engagement. This is great if you have great managers, but it requires a tremendous amount of energy on their part and often results in leadership burnout. I have one client who has relied on manager hyperactivity to drive employee motivation. When I was meeting with this manager about developing new plans, every fifteen minutes or so he'd jump up and run out of his office, go around the brokerage floor clapping, praising, and generally firing up the staff. His enthusiasm was infectious and you could tell the employees loved working for him. But how long could he keep this up? He must go home exhausted. When you have incentive compensation, even when it's a relatively small amount of pay (10–20 percent of total compensation), it gives employees a sense of control and ownership. This will not matter to all employees, but if you can release 25 percent discretionary effort from 50 percent of your employees, you will have increased productivity by 12.5 percent. I know many companies that would be more than happy with a 12.5 percent increase to their bottom line.

Let me add a word of caution on adding incentives to the 100-percent-base salary model. You need to take care when modeling your costs to ensure the incentive kicks in at an *attainable* level of performance that also represents increased performance over the prior year, or your cost of compensation as a percent of profit will increase. But you may be in a position where you need to make this investment—if, for example, you are losing employees because of pay, or you know your pay is below market because you have done a market pay analysis by using a compensation survey such as the one provided by the Transportation

Intermediaries Association (TIA). In this case, adding incentive pay to bring your total pay closer to market will ensure increases only go to the top performers.

Now let's look at the other end of the spectrum—the 100-percent-variable plan. Many of you know this plan well; it typically involves a draw, to cover the employee's basic household expenses, which is deduced from the incentive. If you carry a negative balance forward to the next period, this is called a "recoverable draw." If you do not carry it forward, it's called a "non-recoverable draw." The recoverable draw is the most motivational (if you consider terror a good form of motivation) and is generally found in organizations that have very high turnover. A recoverable draw will also not satisfy the minimum salary test if your organization is reviewing roles for FLSA exempt versus non-exempt status, which means an inside sales role paid this way *must* be paid for overtime regardless of how much money they make from their incentive.

The non-recoverable draw is a salary in disguise. In this case, the salary is used as a threshold, which must be "covered" before incentive pay is earned. This is less terror-inducing, as there is at least some guaranteed pay, but you can never reward an employee through an increase in the draw amount without a corresponding takeaway on the incentive side. It's far better to decouple the two and offer a salary and an incentive plan that has a threshold level of performance which is tied to the economic cost of having the employee in the organization, but which does not automatically increase when a raise is given.

Once companies have taken this step, they often realize that the economic cost of an employee is far more than 1× salary. It is not uncommon to see estimates of 2–3× salary when you factor in benefits, employer-paid taxes, car allowances or other perks, electricity, support staff, etc. Each company should use its own formula based on its unique economics and not assume that because Company X uses 2.5× salary, that is the right answer for everyone. If you provide exceptional benefits, your cost might be 3×. If you provide very few benefits and the employee works from home, your cost might be barely 1.2×. Once you have an understanding of the general economic cost of an employee, get over the need to be accurate *to the penny* about the cost of each employee. Some will cost more and some will cost less. All you need is a guide. You can then set the threshold for compensation from this guide so that all employees in a given role have a threshold that roughly covers their cost. While many companies do, you should not hardwire the two numbers together and tell employees they need to cover 2.5× their salary before they earn incentives. That eliminates a psychological tool—salary increases. If the incentive threshold is hardwired to the salary, then no salary reward comes without an incentive punishment, just as we saw with the non-recoverable draw.

Keep in mind throughout this book, human psychology is varied. What is meaningful to one person is not meaningful to another (see appendix A for a personal story on just how true this can be—even when the subjects in question come from the same gene pool), and business owners, in particular, can have a hard time understanding that employees are not wired as they are. Here's a hint: if they were wired like you, they'd own their own company. Rejoice in this difference, because without it, you'd have a very lonely office.

So if we take it as a given that employees are not wired like owners, you can identify some obvious differences. They will be less risk-averse, need more external recognition and camaraderie, care more about titles and positions of authority, and value having a life outside of work (owners live and breathe their work, and often are perplexed and perturbed that their employees do not do the same). Within your employee population, you know there are some people who are simply not motivated by money. You could tell them that if they stayed until 5:05 p.m. one day, you would give them $1,000—and they would not do it, because whatever they are doing instead is more valuable to them. This person, however, might be a great manager and be motivated to higher levels of performance by being given a team to run. They might still leave at 5:00, but now they have their cell phone with them and are willing to call in to help manage staff after they are physically gone. Other people are motivated by increases in title, so creating role levels such as Carrier Sales I, II, and III can provide motivational value in addition to any corresponding pay increase. For others, motivation may come from an improvement in office or parking space, a casual-dress work environment, a traveling trophy or gift card, or extra time off. You need to be able to use all motivational tools at your disposal, and completely eliminating salary (the 100-percent-variable model) or incentives (the 100-percent-salary model) is taking away one of the most powerful psychological tools in your toolkit for driving employee motivation.

Chapter 5

Selecting the Right Pay Mix: A Question of Prominence

The previous chapter discussed the perils of having a 100 percent salary plan or a 100 percent variable plan, but this raises a question: What is the *right* pay mix? If 100 percent of either is no good, then how much of an employee's pay should be in salary and how much should be incentive? I will answer as a true consultant: "It depends." It depends on the role we are talking about and the level of prominence that role has in effecting change.

Prominence is a tricky word when used in this context. It's a good English word that sales compensation consultants co-opted about fifty years ago to use to mean "ability to make an impact." Often people think it's better to be more prominent, but there really is no value connotation to term. It's not good or bad; it's simply descriptive of the amount of influence in the sales process. It also bears no relation to the amount of total compensation set for the role, as this example should show. A door-to-door vacuum cleaner sales rep is a highly prominent role, but the account manager at Microsoft who handles the Dell account is a less-prominent role. The account manager will certainly make more money than the vacuum cleaner sales rep, but more personal energy, effort, sheer charisma and negotiating power are required to sell those vacuums than for Microsoft to retain Dell as a customer.

In the world of sales, you can break down roles between hunter- and farmer-type roles. Often this gets reduced to a perspective that "hunting is all that matters," but this is far from true. Farmers are equally valuable (perhaps more so, because without them the business would go under very quickly) and need to be valued for the role they play in the organization. But they should not be compensated as hunters—or vice-versa. These are two different roles with two very different prominence levels. Hunters are high-prominence; farmers are lower-prominence. This means only that hunters should have more pay at risk than farmers do, which aligns pay with the ability of the individual in the role to control the outcome.

Carrier sales roles are typically less prominent than either of the two main shipper sales roles, but often are compensated as 100-percent-variable. This causes psychological stress; there are significant portions of the pure carrier-sales role that are outside of the carrier reps' control (two biggies being the type of freight solicited and the price negotiated for that freight). If the sales rep is doing a miserable job, the carrier sales rep downstream will be stuck trying to make a silk purse out of a sow's ear. How fair is it to compensate them based entirely on the quality of the purse produced? Now, some of you may be saying you want back-pressure from carrier sales on shipper sales to drive them to make better deals (or potentially jump them in the parking lot), but this can be handled within the bounds of a *reasonably* variable compensation plan for this role. Of course, it all comes down to the degree of control—prominence. Can the carrier sales role change the outcome (short of threats)? Are they expected to call customers to solicit freight? In this case, it is not a pure carrier sales role, but more a hybrid role, which would indicate a more variable pay mix. How closely do the teams work together? Is the carrier sales role on a very tightly-knit pod or in a pool of resources fighting each other for the same freight? If the latter, then the role is actually more prominent, as now the field is more level and there is equal ability to affect the outcome. If the role is pod-dependent, then there is less ability to affect the outcome.

As you move away from the core sales and operations roles, you find yourself moving into a realm of less prominence and less variability. Order entry, track-and-trace, team leaders, managers, and back office staff are all less prominent than the core individual-contributor roles found in sales and operations. When looking at the hierarchical levels of sales and operational roles for pay mix, there tends to be an hourglass design, with lower-level roles having more pay at risk (more prominent); middle managers having less; but then senior leaders and executives expanding back out for more pay at risk. This makes sense if you think about it. Middle managers execute senior leaders' directives through the people they manage. They may be fantastic at what they do, but it would be very hard to tell specifically, as the majority of their work is accomplished through others. Senior leaders, on the other hand, set policy and direction, make critical health-of-business decisions, and can make or break the entire organization. They should have more pay at risk, just not so much that they are tempted to commit fraud—we've all seen where that ends up.

So what is the "right" mix? It depends. But some good guidelines are as follows:

Table 5.1: *Example Pay Mixes by Common Roles and Their Impacts*

Pay Mix[7] (Salary/Incentive)	Commonly Used For	Impact on Individual and Company
0/100	Pure hunter sales	Not recommended due to the high level of stress; if used, the company must accept and desire a high degree of independence from the people in the role; monthly or weekly payouts are required for employee cash flow; I call this a "timeshare" or "used car" sales rep plan.
50/50	Hunter sales or hunter-farmer blends	Most variable plan recommended; allows company to give direction and yet highly motivational; monthly payouts required for employee cash flow.
60/40	Account managers who have the ability to influence add-on, up-sales, or new orders	Still meaningful enough to be highly motivational; incentive portion starting to be small enough that it could be paid quarterly but monthly may still be best.
70/30	Carrier sales	Provides the best balance of base salary security to account for things outside of their control, with a meaningful incentive plan to drive behavior (consider that with this mix, the incentive is 43 percent of the salary).
80/20	Sales and operations support roles	A level with small enough variability that it is OK to consider 100 percent team based plans; quarterly payouts (or even annual) will likely be OK.
90/10	Back-office staff	These plans provide limited true motivation—it's more about being part of the team and not having the staff feel left out. It can also be a way to hedge your bets against a bad year, as 10 percent of your admin staff costs are now tied to company performance. Best not to pay too frequently as the amount will be too small to be meaningful: semi-annual or annual might be best.

[7] Pay mix is represented as two whole numbers in relation to one another. A 70/30 pay mix means 70 percent of the Target Total Compensation (TTC) is salary and 30 percent is incentive.

When considering the optimal pay mix for the roles in your organization, you must also think about things like brand recognition. Working for a major company that everyone knows and respects gives you a leg up on the competitor who works for Company No-Name, so the major company rep has less direct work to do to gain business and is therefore less prominent than a rep at an unknown or a start-up. Think too about support systems: CRM, marketing materials, lead generation from support staff or management—all of the things that can make a sales rep's job either easy or a living nightmare. The more frustration the rep will have, the less pay you should put at risk. The smoother the operations flow, the more pay can be on the line because the rep's ability to sell is now the only barrier to success.

Use pay mix and prominence with caution. As with many things in life, more is not always better. While CFOs love the use of variable pay throughout the organization, doing this in the extreme will create a dysfunctional organization with considerable role confusion, animosity, and a detrimental level of competitiveness. The trick is to find the right balance of pay mix among the roles to support the culture you are trying to engender.

Chapter 6

But How Much Should We Pay? Using Compensation Surveys to Set Target Total Compensation

Discussing pay mix is all well and good, but how do you know you are paying a competitive TTC (Target Total Compensation)? Salary surveys can be a very useful tool to help answer this question, but you have to know how to use them.

Everyone's got a compensation fish story. "Every dispatcher at so-and-so company makes at least $150,000 per year covering freight." "I hear that so-and-so is paying salary plus 30 percent commission." Or worse, a highly qualified and seemingly desirable prospective employee swears he or she is worth triple what you are really willing to pay. How do you sort out fact from fiction to determine whether you are paying market competitive wages or are getting left in the dust?

My first bit of advice is to use common sense. There are exceptions to every rule, but how likely do you think it is the high earnings you are hearing reported are representative of the industry—even for a single company? What is more likely is that you are hearing about one stand-out case that may have special circumstances attached to it.

My second bit of advice is to arm yourself with some facts. Get some data. Now, this needs to be done properly, as the United States Department of Justice (DOJ) frowns on companies or organizations that price-fix wages by comparing pay levels, and many associations or companies have gotten in hot water by not following the DOJ guidelines. So first you should be aware that there are regulations regarding how compensation surveys must be run. Here are the rules (as of 2016):

1. The survey must be administered by an unaffiliated third party (e.g., government agency, consultant, industry association, or academic institution) who can hold the data private (so one company can't collect the data on a set of peers and then report the results out to the group).

2. The data must be at least three months old (meaning if the data are from December 31 you should not be seeing any reports using that data until the following April).

3. There must be five companies represented in any disseminated statistic (i.e., "cut" of the data).

4. No single company can represent 25 percent or more of the sample size (so

one company can't skew the results). Combining rule #4 with rule #3 can make a statistic not reportable pretty quickly, let me tell you.

It's not uncommon for companies to sponsor custom salary surveys with a narrowly defined target peer group ("I want to know how these five companies pay these seven roles in rural Pennsylvania"). But recognize that custom surveys have at best a 30 percent response rate, and even if you did manage to get five companies to respond, they would all need to have the same positions in that geography to see any meaningful results. For a useful survey, you will need to cast your net wider—target at least twenty to thirty companies, and define job matches as broadly as reasonable in a larger geographic area to get the best results.

I can hear you saying it now: "But jobs don't pay the same in New York or Atlanta as they do in rural Mississippi." And you are right, they don't. But there are plenty of studies that define geographic differentials, so you can easily take a national statistic and calibrate it to your specific market. You will also find that geographic differentials are not that extreme, and differences in pay may be driven by experience differences among individuals, benefits offered (worse benefits = higher cash compensation), or perceived stability of the company (big, stable companies can get away with paying less). There may be isolated markets, such as exceedingly small towns, where the geographic difference from the national average is greater, but you will know if you are in one of those markets and will probably have a better handle on your market pay level than any survey can provide.

In order for you to understand how to interpret the data reported from a survey, I need to spend a minute going over some basic statistical terms, so bear with me. Many people do not realize there is a profound difference between the average (or mean) and median, and that it's important to always look at the median when reviewing pay levels. A simple example should suffice. Take the table of salaries below:

Table 6.1: *Finding the Median Salary*

Annual Salaries of Account Executives
$150,000
$60,000
$45,000
$38,000
$37,500
$36,000
$36,000
$32,000
$28,000

The mean, or average, salary for this population is $51,388 (the sum of all salaries, divided by 9). But you can clearly see it would be misleading to state that $51,000 is the market pay for an Account Executive, and it's certainly not $150,000. Instead, locate the median (middle entry) of the data set, which is $37,500. Half of the population is paid more than this amount and half is paid less. This is a more reasonable representation of market-competitive wages.

The median is also referred to as the 50th percentile; on a bell curve distribution of data points, it marks the middle. There are two other points to note: the 25th percentile and the 75th percentile. In the table above, the 25th percentile is $36,000 and the 75th percentile is $45,000. This is not a big spread, which means the data points are going to be pretty closely clustered around the median. If the 25th percentile were $20,000 and the 75th percentile were $80,000, then you would know there is a wide variation between the salary levels reported.

In Excel, you can figure these statistics using these formulas:

- *=Percentile*(array,.25) for the 25th percentile

- *=Percentile*(array,.50) for the 50th percentile (median)

- *=Percentile*(array,.75) for the 75th percentile

  Note: *array* is the data set you are analyzing, e.g., A1:A30 if your data are in column A rows 1 to 30.

Try running these stats on your daily load counts or daily gross profit totals from the last month, as you may find some interesting things about what is really happening in your company. For the same reasons noted above, using an average for these data points, especially on smaller sets of numbers, can be misleading.

As a side note, whenever you are calibrating performance ranges for your incentive plan, you should look at your historical average, median, 25th, and 75th percentiles to get a true understanding of realistic performance expectations. If the average and the median are far off from one another, then you should dig for the outlier to understand what happened to cause the anomaly. Then you should set your target performance expectation around the 60th percentile so people are stretched to do a bit more than they've typically done in the past. Think about this; if your new 50th percentile is what was the 60th percentile in the prior year, that would be around a *10 percent gain in overall productivity as your bell curve will have shifted 10 points to the right* at all levels of performance.

Given the above statistics review, it should be clear why you should exercise extreme caution using a survey that reports *averages* rather than *medians*, as you'll really have no idea what the data are actually telling you. Similarly, check to see how the data are gathered, as you want surveys that gather data at the employee or incumbent level. You can tell when this is the case because the survey should report two statistics along with every data cut:

- The number of companies in the sample (and it should never be fewer than five for any statistic; if the total number of companies who provided data for the survey is less than five or if you are able to identify any specific company's data, delete the survey and run the other direction as your participation in it could land you in hot water with the DOJ as this is considered "price fixing")

- The number of employees in the sample (often abbreviated as N, or FTE for "Full-Time Equivalent" when part-time employees have been "normed" to full-time rates)

If the number of employees is not reported or is always identical to the number of companies, then you need to check the survey methodology. If a survey administrator asks each company to provide the average pay level for their employees in a role (one data point per company per role), and then reports the average of these findings across companies, just imagine how far that data can be skewed away from the true reality! Given that there are some instances of exceedingly high pay levels in this industry (I know, because I've seen the data), this is a significant risk and can result in companies wasting precious dollars paying far more than they need to for the type of talent they want. And, I guarantee your employees aren't going to tell you they are overpaid.

Last but not least, you should recognize that you will need to give in order to get. Good surveys typically require a one-time or annual fee, with firms running the big general industry surveys charging thousands of dollars per year. Yes, there are free surveys out there, but running a survey to the DOJ rule-compliance standards requires significant programming skill to run recursive tests on the data, staff to scrub the data and follow up with companies to resolve "bad data" issues rather than letting it through with an "oh well, that's what they reported" attitude, and significant marketing effort to maximize participation. None of this comes free. Also, typically if you want to access survey data, you are going to need to give your data to the survey administrator. Surveys can be incredibly valuable tools, and they become exponentially more valuable the more data is collected. When many companies have provided data, it becomes possible to start cutting data by job, level, geography, company size, and maybe even type of freight. But that is only possible with significantly high levels of participation by companies in the industry.

Chapter 7

Using Leverage to Maximize Motivation

Now let's turn to some of the most exciting concepts of incentive design—upside, downside, leverage, and dispersion.

The upside is the amount of pay that a top performer can earn, and downside—well—you can guess that one. It's how much risk there is on the downside for a poor performer. Leverage refers to the plan design ratio for the top 10 percent (decile) performer relative to the median performer, and dispersion refers to the amount of leverage that a plan actually achieves. So let's unpack these one at a time.

Generally speaking, you want your team's performance on your incentive plan to result in a bell curve, with the following "look":

Table 7.1: *Model Incentive Plan Bell Curve*

- No more than 10 percent of employees should be below threshold (the minimum acceptable level of attainment on the plan, which often means they are earning no incentive pay)

- 50 percent to 60 percent of the employees should be earning at or above target (the expected payout level for hitting quota, or goal, which is tied to market-competitive pay and your desired pay mix for the role)

- About 10 percent of the employees should be at or above excellence (a really good level of performance that you wish *everyone* in your organization could hit but that you know only a few will attain)

The amount of pay you tie to each of these marker points determines the motivational value of your plan. If you pay $1,000 for reaching quota, and you pay $0 for just below threshold, then the downside of your plan is $0. If you have a straight-line commission with no threshold, then your plan has no real downside, as moving even one load will result in some incentive pay. If your overall plan has a base salary in place, then your plan should have a threshold that has a meaningful downside. Typically, I recommend paying roughly 25 percent of the target incentive (in this example, that would be $250) when threshold is reached, but $0 below threshold. You want a bit of a cliff at threshold to encourage as many people to get above threshold as possible. Remember, you want 90 percent of your employees earning above threshold pay. Those who are below threshold for too many pay cycles are probably not long for the company.

The amount you pay at excellence is your leverage factor, and this typically should be two to three times the pay at target. So, if your target incentive compensation (TIC) is $1,000, then your pay at excellence should be $2,000 to $3,000. This ratio is generally determined by the amount of pay at risk and how difficult it is to reach excellence. If you have more pay at risk for the role (for example, a 50/50 pay mix), then you should have a 3× leverage factor (or possibly more). If you have an 80/20 pay mix, then a 2× leverage factor is just fine. For admin staff with a 90/10 pay mix, 1.5× may be plenty. Setting this marker helps you determine a variety of things about your plan mechanics (and yes, you should have this discussion before you even know what you are measuring or how you are going to do the calculations—it acts as a philosophical guide for the rest of the journey). For example, if you have a tiered commission plan, it guides you to the numbers you need to use to ensure the leverage factor is reached at the excellence level. Here is a quick example using a monthly retroactive (back-to-the-first-dollar) commission plan:

- **Threshold** of $15,000 in GP$ should pay $250; rate at $15,000 = 1.67 percent ($250/$15,000)

- **Target** of $25,000 in GP$ should pay $1,000; rate at $25,000 = 4.00 percent ($1,000/$25,000)

- **Excellence** of $40,000 in GP$ should pay $2,000; rate at $40,000 = 5.00 percent ($2,000/$40,000)

  Note: *All dollar amounts are illustrative and are not recommendations about performance and/or pay for any role.*

Now, of course, you need to test the economics to be sure that you can afford to pay 5 percent at $40,000 a month in GP$ (including salary expense).

But notice how this plan creates the motivational drive to want to get to $40,000? The payout is $400 higher than if we'd kept the 4 percent rate on all GP dollars above $25,000. You should set the excellence level at about the point where your top 10 percent performer lands (if you have 100 performers, this would be the 10th from the top). This helps create the bell curve I talked about earlier. Historical performance determines excellence, and then you set the leverage factor to help drive a higher level of pay to your top-10-percent performers. Over time, these marker points will of course change. As you drive your staff to higher levels of performance, you can and should increase what you consider excellence. Keep in mind, however, that infinity is not attainable, and there will come a time when the slope of the performance increase curve starts to taper off. There will be a point of stasis until you change something about your business model, systems, or processes to enable an increase in production.

Upside refers to the amount of pay one can earn at excellence or above, and often helps explain whether a plan has a cap or not. If the upside is unlimited, then there is no cap. If the maximum payout is 3× the target incentive, then in our example, the maximum upside would be $3,000 per month, with an excellence payout of $2,000. So you would tell a recruit that the plan's potential upside would be $2,000 to $3,000 per month. In most cases for brokers, it would be unusual to put a cap on an individual component of an incentive plan (why would you want them to stop moving loads?). There are some industries, however, in which capacity can be limited (e.g., trucking) and it may be in the company's better interest to limit the amount of total sales and focus instead on getting more of the right *type* of sales.

The last concept to cover is dispersion. This refers to an after-the-fact check on the health of your incentive plan. All it takes is a simple Excel calculation. On your spreadsheet that lists all incentive payouts for employees (do not include salary payments), group employees by role (so all inside sales are together, all carrier sales are together, etc.), and then apply this formula to the incentive payouts for a single role:

=Percentile(A1:A30,.90)/*percentile*(A1:A30,.50)

Note: *Substitute the actual cell range location in your workbook of the incentive payouts for A1:A30 in the above formula; in your case, it may be D10:D567, depending on how your data are arranged and how many employees you have in a role.*

This formula divides the 50th percentile incentive payout into the 90th percentile incentive payout and the result should be a number between 1 and 5. In my experience, it's highly likely that it will be between 1 and 1.5 because most incentive plans do not have enough leverage in the design or they have a goal setting problem (or both). What this calculation tells you is the ratio between the top 10 percent performer's pay and the median performer's pay. If you designed your plan to have a 3× payout at excellence, and your dispersion is 1.25, then you have a problem. Either the median level of attainment is too high (and your costs are probably running amok), or the excellence level is set too high for people to actually reach it (and your plan is not providing the motivational value it should). One of the most common problems with 100-percent-variable plans is a lack of dispersion. This is because so much of the incentive is actually serving the function of a base salary: providing the employee with steady enough income to allow for house and car payments. It can also be problematic to have too much dispersion. If your ratio is more than 7, then you may not be using a valid goal-setting or expectation-setting approach, or you may be using the wrong type of plan design for the role, resulting in unreasonably high payouts for some members of your team. For example, it may be that they have house accounts or other types of freight that are easier to move, but are being paid the same as difficult spot-market freight. You may think this is not a problem, but that high-end payout, if perceived as out-of-reach for the masses or unjustly earned, may actually create a toxic environment for the bulk of your employees. Furthermore, these "super-rich" top performers often create a barrier for management, keeping them from making sound business decisions that would be in the best interest of the entire company out of fear of losing these performers and their accounts.

In summary, in order to gain motivation from the incentive plan, you want it to be *truly* variable, with meaningful upside and downside that reward top performers while encouraging bottom performers to work hard to move themselves up the curve.

Chapter 8

Selecting the Right Performance Measures for Your Incentive Plan

Now, since we have a pretty good idea of *how much* to pay, we need to consider what it is you are paying for. It is not, or should not be, as simple as just paying for gross profit, as you probably need different types of gross profit to run your business. You need gross profit from existing customers, and you need gross profit from new customers. You need gross profit that maximizes your network and minimizes your cost to serve. If you only pay your employees for any gross profit dollars that walk in the door, you may find you are getting gross profit dollars that are pretty wrinkly and worn out, when you'd really rather get some nice new crisp bills in hand. So, how to decide what to use in your incentive plan?

In chapter 3 we talked about the importance of planning, setting goals, developing a clear strategy for achieving these goals, and aligning your organization structure to support these objectives. Now we need to get into the nitty gritty of role accountabilities and expectations, as you cannot simply say, "everyone is responsible for everything." You *must* have role clarity, and you must keep accountabilities to as few as possible per role to drive maximum results. If you ask one person to do ten things, you will never get more than two or three done well, another two to three done more or less OK, and four to six done really poorly. Extrapolate this across your entire staff and ask if you are really OK with 40 percent to 60 percent of critical business activities being done poorly? You need to segment roles to allow people to focus and improve performance in the few areas they are assigned.

A simple exercise can help with this. Write down every title in your organization into a table like this:

Table 8.1: *Example of Role/Accountability/Expectation/Measures*

Role	Accountabilities	Expectations	Measures
The title found on your org chart or job description (*not* the name of a person)	The top four or five primary job responsibilities (why do you have this role?)	Put numbers to the accountabilities—be *specific*!	What you can measure that reinforces the accountabilities?
Example			
Carrier sales	• Cover freight • Generate gross profit • Negotiate with carriers to improve profit • Develop relationships with new carriers to help fill holes • Ensure loads are delivered on time • Work as a team to support each other	• 10–12 loads per day • $38,400 in gross profit per month • Attain $160 GP$ per load on average • Attain average of 16 percent GP% • Develop two new carriers per month who ship at least ten loads	• Individual gross profit $ • Individual GP% • Team load count

Note: *all numbers are illustrative and will vary dramatically by type of freight, experience level of the role, and company specifics. Do not adapt these numbers directly for your staff as they will likely be wrong.*

Then, as you can see in the example, fill in each section, starting with *accountabilities* and working your way to the right. You should not have more than ten bullets in the accountabilities section—preferably less. This is not a complete job description, but the top few things that you fundamentally expect this role to accomplish (not all the details about how they accomplish these results). Expectations are the numbers that go with the accountabilities. Ask: How many? How often? What kind? For sales, think about how many new customers are needed, and at what size, to hit your new business growth goal. Is repeat freight from a single customer important? What constitutes repeat freight? Ten loads per week, or ten loads per month, or ten loads per day? What do you need from existing customers? New lanes? New types of freight? Be specific and write down the numbers. This will help immeasurably with the development of your incentive plan.

The last step is to think about what measurable items your list points to: things that matter to the company, are controllable by the person, and can be measured and tracked. Fill in no more than four of these items in the last column. Consider the scope of measurement; will it be at the individual level, team level, or company level? Now step back. You have the beginnings of a really good, balanced compensation plan.

Chapter 9

Assigning Weights to Your Performance Measures

In the last chapter, we ended with the following "Role Accountabilities" table:

Table 9.1: *Original Role/Accountability/Expectation/Measures*

Role	Accountabilities	Expectations	Measures
The title found on your org chart or job description (*not* the name of a person)	The top four or five primary job responsibilities (why do you have this role?)	Put numbers to the accountabilities—be *specific!*	What you can measure that reinforces the accountabilities?
Example			
Carrier sales	• Cover freight • Generate gross profit • Negotiate with carriers to improve profit • Develop relationships with new carriers to help fill holes • Ensure loads are delivered on time • Work as a team to support each other	• 10–12 loads per day • $38,400 in gross profit per month • Attain $160 GP$ per load on average • Attain average of 16 percent GP% • Develop two new carriers per month who ship at least ten loads	• Individual gross profit $ • Individual GP% • Team load count

Defining these details for all of the roles in your organization can be tedious, to say the least, but it is *essential* for a good plan design. It's also essential that you have many heads working on this together. One person cannot think of all angles. For example, something is missing from the Measures part of the table above that looks like it might be pretty important for this role. Can you see it? I've highlighted the miss on the next table.

Table 9.2: *Revised Example of Role/Accountability/Expectation/Measures*

Role	Accountabilities	Expectations	Measures
The title found on your org chart or job description (*not* the name of a person)	The top four or five primary job responsibilities (why do you have this role?)	Put numbers to the accountabilities—be *specific*!	What you can measure that reinforces the accountabilities?
Example			
Carrier sales	• Cover freight • Generate gross profit • Negotiate with carriers to improve profit • Develop relationships with new carriers to help fill holes • Ensure loads are delivered on time • Work as a team to support each other	• 10–12 loads per day • $38,400 in gross profit per month • Attain $160 GP$ per load on average • Attain average of 16 percent GP% • Develop two new carriers per month who ship at least ten loads	• Individual gross profit $ • Individual GP% • New carriers • Team load count

Now we need to focus in on the four things we've identified as *potential* performance measures and see if they make the grade. This is where some horse-trading and compromising comes in, and where your team will have to get aligned with the company priorities. It is this part of the process that delivers 90 percent of the benefit of going through a compensation design project: you are building alignment, focus, and agreement among your leadership team about what is really important for the organization. Not all of your leaders will agree with you. That is OK. Allow time for healthy discussion and debate. Hear different opinions. Gather different ideas. Think broadly and think of new approaches. Put more ideas down rather than less to start. We will weed through them in a minute. You may find some ideas are raised that are not appropriate for use in an incentive plan (number of calls, attendance, etc.), but that may be really good in a performance management plan. Capture them now, so you can use them later in another system. Many of our clients say the work we do together provides more than new compensation plans—it forces alignment, clarity, and focus. It is this part of the process that delivers that magic.

However, you could easily start to feel overwhelmed at this phase (imagine looking at the above table for ten or more roles in your organization—I have worked with companies that have over sixty roles), so you need to use some good project management processes to ensure you stay on track, as well as some guidelines to help you make the trade-off decisions to pare down your measures for a good solid incentive plan. Here are the rules:

- Good performance measures are:

  - Relevant (what you are measuring matters to the business)

  - Objective (anyone can determine "good" or "bad" performance based on numbers; it is not based on the subjective opinion of a leader)

  - Measurable (you can, or better yet, already do, track results from this measure)

  - Controllable (the role impacts the outcome of this measure and the people in the role have a clear "line of sight" to how their performance changes the result)

- There should be no more than four weighted measures (three is better).

- Nothing should be weighted less than 20 percent of the total.

Sometimes it's helpful to look at what *doesn't* work to understand what each rule means:

- **Number of phone calls** is the classic measure that fails the **relevancy** test. For any call center environment, which most brokerages are, number of outbound phone calls is an objective, measurable, and controllable measure. But it is not particularly relevant in and of itself. Phone calls are a means to an end, but not an end that should be paid for. If you put number of phone calls in your incentive plan, you will get a lot of phone calls—but you may not get any loads, and your plan economics will be out of whack.

- **Attitude** is a commonly suggested measure that fails the **objectivity** test. It is critical to a business's health to not have grouches around, but one person's grouch is another person's pragmatist. This kind of measure should be used very sparingly, if at all, in the incentive plan. It's much more commonly found in an annual performance review discussion.

- **Yield** is a great measure that many trucking companies would like to use, but have tremendous difficulty **measuring**. If you need to hire a team of programmers to develop the measure, and there is considerable argument about how it should be calculated (just ask any two trucking executives how yield should be calculated and you will see what I mean), then you may not be ready to include this measure in the incentive plan.

- **Earnings Before Interest, Taxes, Depreciation and Amortization (EBITDA) or Operating Income** certainly satisfies the first three requirements, but falls down on **controllability** for most roles in the organization. Profit-sharing plans are great, and serve a wonderful purpose in an organization, but they are not the same thing as an incentive plan—and the two should never be confused. If you plan to tie all of your employees to operating income as their only incentive, don't expect to see much change in their behavior because impacting the result is too far outside of their control.

Applying these rules should help you eliminate some measures. Now you need to deal with the next two rules: No more than four, no less than 20 percent on each. Let's recap one minute on what is meant by 20 percent (20 percent of *what*?).

You established the role's Target Total Compensation (TTC)[8] based on the market value of the job, and set pay mix (how much is salary/how much is incentive) based on the prominence of the role and the culture of the company. Let's say for example (*don't take examples as gospel—each company is different*), that for an entry-level carrier sales role, you set TTC at $48,000 with salary midpoint at $36,000 ($28k[9] to $43k range, minimum to maximum) and Target Incentive Compensation (TIC) at $12,000 with 3× upside (leverage). This is a 75/25 pay mix. An outstanding performer could triple the payout to earn $36,000 in incentive (3 × $12,000) for $72,000 total pay. But you need to first allocate the target incentive ($12,000) and define how this will be earned. This is where the measures come in. The accountabilities table made it clear there are four key things to focus the incentive plan on for this role:

- Individual gross profit $

- Individual GP percent (GP%)

- New carriers

- Team load count

These are going to be the four things that drive the incentive payout, but only three of them need to carry weight (a modifier does not carry its own weight—it is secondary to another element and GP% is commonly used as a modifier to another element). Chapter 14 will give you more insights into the various forms and uses of modifiers.

So, how much of the $12,000 target incentive do you want to allocate to each of the three weighted elements? (If we do this in percentages, it makes it easier to deal with many roles at one time that have different target incentive amounts. The allocations need to add to 100 percent, and no element can get less than 20 percent.)

- Individual GP$ with individual GP% modifier

- New carriers

- Team load count

---

[8] All numbers given are annual numbers.

[9] For non-exempt roles, it is a good idea to be sure your lowest salary level exceeds the minimum wage x 2,080 hours for your state or locality. While it is possible for outside sales roles to be 100% variable (no salary and no OT requirements) most brokerage roles do not meet the duties test for being truly "outside sales" and therefore are subject to FLSA rules on minimum wage and overtime.

Your weights should convey priorities. As noted in chapter 2, putting something in an incentive plan is like putting a megaphone on it. Be sure your megaphone is saying the right things. It's unlikely that all pieces are the same in importance, so I often add another rule: weights cannot be the same (25/25/25/25 for four measures, or 33/33/34 for three measures, or 50/50 for 2 measures). On occasion, I allow this rule to be broken, but you have to know when and where this is OK.

I will leave you at this point to debate among your team how to allocate the incentive among these three measures, and we'll pick back up at this point in our next section.

SECTION III

The Care and Feeding of Your Beast

Chapter 10

Moving from Measures to Design Details

Small freight brokers whose team relies heavily on one another for coverage may place a higher premium on teamwork than larger brokers who desire each team member to display a high degree of individual competitiveness. These brokers may, in fact, throw out the team load-count goal entirely: "We don't need no stinkin' teamwork," they might say; "It's all about the individual!" And for them, that is exactly what they should do. But for others, it's entirely the wrong answer.

For the sake of our example, we'll assume that you have a medium-sized brokerage (thirty to seventy-five employees); there are some carrier pods in place, perhaps organized by region or by freight type; and they provide some coverage for one another, so teamwork is important.

While you were debating the value of teamwork with your partner, your sales manager and operations manager have been having a healthy debate over using load count as a measure at all. The conversation has proceeded along these lines:

Sales Manager: "Why in the world would we pay for load count? Your carrier salespeople will cover the load for nothing just to get the credit and my reps will get [expletive] out of their gross profit credit."

Operations Manager: "We have to give load-count credit because my team ends up having to cover the crap loads that your sales team sells. We can't turn it away because we need the customer relationship for the good freight, but until your team learns to explain to the customers that not all loads can be covered at the same price, we can't have the ops team working this hard for nothing."

You jump into the fray to help calm both sides down. Everyone agrees Gross Profit $ is the most important measure and should have at least 50 percent of the plan weight, but the Sales Manager wants nothing on load count, and the Ops Manager wants as much as possible. The Sales Manager's vote would be 60 percent on GP$ and 40 percent on new carriers, based on the argument that more new carriers will make it easier to get freight from new customers. The Ops Manager's vote is 50 percent on GP$, 20 percent on new carriers, and 30 percent on team load count. In the end, all sides agree to the following:

- GP$ with GP% modifier: 50 percent

- New carriers: 30 percent

- Team load count: 20 percent

As the owner, this may not be exactly how you would have weighted the elements, but you understand that it's important for your leadership team to buy in to the process and the outcome. You can live with it, and, most importantly, so can they. And guess what? You just got sales and ops to agree on *something*.

Now we need to start thinking about plan mechanics. We know what we are going to measure, but *how* are we going to measure it, and how are we going to pay the incentive? There are some critical choices to make when thinking about mechanics, and you should apply the questions to each measure independently. You don't need to answer the same way for all of them. In fact, in many cases, it is better if you don't.

The decisions to be made are outlined below. If a term is unfamiliar, don't worry; the rest of section III covers them all in depth.

DETAILED DESIGN DECISIONS

- **TIC (Target Incentive Compensation) Anchor Point:** Fixed by role, or percent of salary or midpoint?

- **Goal Setting Approach:** Absolute (common for all) versus relative (unique by person or group)?

- **Payment Method:** Percent-of-volume, or percent-of-TIC?

- **Scope:** What level of aggregation is used in the measure (i.e., when we say team, what team?)?

- **Crediting Point:** When is a load a load for the plan: pickup, delivery, invoice, payment, or some other point that makes sense for your company?

- **Performance Period:** What time horizon do you want to use: monthly, quarterly, annually?

- **Pay Frequency:** How often do you want (or need) to make incentive payments? This is not the same thing as performance period, as you can use an annual goal, but make monthly payments against progress toward that goal.

- **Performance Ranges:** What constitutes minimal acceptable performance (threshold), target performance, and excellence?

- **Use of caps or decelerators:** Are they necessary? How good is your crystal ball?

- **Use of qualifiers, modifiers, kickers, depressors, and cross-gates:** What protections need to be in place?

There are a few global questions that also need to be addressed, and these will apply to all measures and likely all roles. These are:

- Crediting Rules: Who gets credit for a load? Based on what code in your TMS system? What if more than one person touches a load (as is often the case)? How do you make sure you aren't overpaying? What field in your TMS applies to each role, and when might there be exceptions to this?

- Chargebacks, clawbacks, and holdbacks: The ugly, the uglier, and the illegal.

- Vacation, sick time or PTO: How to account for incentive payouts when someone is out of the office? (And no, having them never take time off is not a reasonable answer).

I will address the first detailed design decision in this chapter, and the other answers can be found later in section III.

TIC Anchor Point: Fixed by Role, Percent-of-Salary or Midpoint?

This question determines how you are going to calculate and communicate the target incentive. There are essentially two choices. You can tell everyone in a given role (for example, our sample carrier salesperson role) that his or her target incentive for the year is $12,000. Or you could tell everyone that his or her target incentive is 33 percent of his or her salary. (A 75/25 pay mix is the same as having 33 percent of salary in incentive, simply divide the second number into the first (25 is 33 percent of 75) to get the incentive as percent of salary.) You would do this if you had very different salary levels for people in the same role and you wanted the incentive to have the same relative importance to everyone ($12k means a lot more to someone with a $30k salary than it does to someone with a $70k salary). You may also need to take this approach if you want to maintain consistency within a corporate grade level and incentive target structure that exists elsewhere in the organization.

Generally speaking, a fixed-dollar target by role (e.g., $12,000 for everyone who is in the Carrier Sales I role) is the better option for roles that have a direct and significant influence on revenue or profit generation, provided there is some rationality to your salary structure. The benefits of a fixed-dollar target incentive are myriad:

- It can neutralize inequities in salary that have crept into your system rather than amplify them.

- It makes budgeting much easier.

- It allows you to manage two of the motivational levers (salary and incentive pay) independently of one another (when incentive is a percent of salary, any salary increase also brings an incentive increase).

- It opens the door for certain mechanics that are nearly impossible under a percent-of-salary approach (such as commissions, banks and bounties).

- It makes it easier to communicate the plans.

- If salaries don't vary that much, using a fixed-dollar target incentive is practically the same thing as using a percent-of-salary approach from an individual pay mix perspective.

In the next chapter, we will go over how to determine your goal setting approach: absolute (same expectation for all) or relative (unique goals) and how to decide the calculation methodology (as a percent of revenue or profit, or as a percent of a target incentive).

Chapter 11

Understanding Goal and Payment Options

In our last chapter, we assigned weights to measures and determined that using a fixed-dollar target (such as $12,000) was the best approach for communicating the target incentive (rather than communicating the target incentive as 33 percent of salary).

We are working our way through the detailed design decisions (see sidebar) and we will tackle the next two decisions in this chapter: Goal Setting Approach and Payment Method.

By far, the number one problem with incentive plans involves goal-setting. It is not that goals are set too high or too low, but that they are *not really set at all*. When goals are not used, everyone is held to a common expectation (an absolute goal) and inequity may develop in the system. Using an absolute goal can work in some cases, but these are very limited and often have an expiration date. The classic example of absolute goals not working is the example of a sales rep in New York and a sales rep in South Dakota. Unless they are selling farm equipment, the New York rep will have an inherent advantage over the South Dakota rep. If the New York rep sells twice as much as the South Dakota rep, does it really mean the New York rep is twice as good? Of course not. It just means there is twice as much opportunity in New York. Does the New York rep really deserve twice as much money? The South Dakota rep may be doing a *phenomenal* job, but if she is held to the same expectation as the New York rep, neither you nor she will ever feel she is doing a good job, and her pay likely will not reflect the effort put forth.

The solution is, of course, to set *relative* goals and pay for goal attainment rather than, or in addition to, volume. This would mean the South Dakota rep's annual sales goal is $1 million and the New York rep's goal is $2 million. You have now set attainable goals for the South Dakota rep, and you and she will know when she is doing a good job, *and* you have also set a realistic goal for

DETAILED DESIGN DECISIONS

- **TIC (Target Incentive Compensation) Anchor Point:** Fixed by role, or percent of salary or midpoint?

- **Goal Setting Approach:** Absolute (common for all) versus relative (unique by person or group)?

- **Payment Method:** Percent-of-volume, or percent-of-TIC?

- **Scope:** What level of aggregation is used in the measure (i.e., when we say team, what team?)?

- **Crediting Point:** When is a load a load for the plan: pickup, delivery, invoice, payment, or some other point that makes sense for your company?

- **Performance Period:** What time horizon do you want to use: monthly, quarterly, annually?

- **Pay Frequency:** How often do you want (or need) to make incentive payments? This is not the same thing as performance period, as you can use an annual goal, but make monthly payments against progress toward that goal.

- **Performance Ranges:** What constitutes minimal acceptable performance (threshold), target performance, and excellence?

- **Use of caps or decelerators:** Are they necessary? How good is your crystal ball?

- **Use of qualifiers, modifiers, kickers, depressors, and cross-gates:** What protections need to be in place?

the New York rep, so he will no longer have a false sense of accomplishment or be overpaid for easy work, but realize effort is required to exceed the goal he's been given.

Absolute goals (the same numerical goal for both the New York and South Dakota reps) only work if there is a completely level playing field. For many brokerages, this is the case at least initially, as there are no geographic boundaries to limit opportunity. Over time, however, situations arise that make the playing field unequal. A rep may leave the company and leave accounts behind that need to be looked after. Or an outside sales rep lands an account that needs to be handed to an inside rep. In an absolute-goal environment, being the person who doles out these accounts is like being Santa Claus. Some firms go to considerable effort to create systems to ensure equality of opportunity, from phone routing rules to account assignment rules and elaborate systems of "account protection." When the system becomes unwieldy, and reps are spending more time managing existing accounts than hunting for new ones, it may be time to consider using relative goals. The initial step is to set relative goals by level, type of freight, or type of account, but to maintain absolute goals for all reps within the sub-group. For very large organizations, this may be the only option that makes sense. For smaller organizations (or ones with excellent management discipline), setting relative (unique) goals for each person is entirely possible and may be the only way to solve the incentive problems that develop from the use of absolute goals.

The second part of the discussion is so intertwined with the first, it's nearly impossible to think about them separately. But they are in fact separate decision points. This is the decision whether to pay for volume (percent-of-revenue or percent-of-profit) or to pay using a percent-of-target incentive approach. Normally, absolute goals and percent-of-volume payment schemes (commissions[10]) go hand-in-hand. This is called a "Cost-of-Sales" philosophy and resonates with most CFOs and financial-purist types. The decision is made about how much can be paid for the sales resource (e.g., 10 percent of gross profit) and this becomes the commission rate paid to all reps, regardless of opportunity, skill, freight type, account history, market value of the job, or sometimes even common sense. The biggest problem with this approach is it wastes money. First, paying purely for volume often results in overpaying the market value of the job. Second, and most importantly, owners never get the appropriate ROI on investments in business improvement systems. Have you upgraded your TMS system, added a marketing team, a CRM system, or bought a big ad in *Transport Topics*? All of these things cost the business money, but if you use a straight-commission approach to incentives, your sales reps reap the reward without incurring any of the costs

---

[10] "Commission" is a problematic word as it generally carries two meanings. The technical definition of a commission is a mathematical method that pays using a percent of a dollar generated (usually revenue or profit). The commonly used meaning of "commission" is as a general term for any incentive payments made that are not salary. I often hear clients refer to "salary plus commission" whether they are paying using a commission mechanic or not. Given the California legislation about documenting true commission plans (see chapter 2) I recommend avoiding the word commission except when you are describing the calculation method, and using the term "incentive" instead for non-salary pay. Therefore, "salary plus incentive" is a better way to describe a pay method that uses both fixed and variable pay.

unless you are making deductions from their profit credit as "charges" for these services, but this gets very confusing and confrontational quickly.

The other end of the spectrum is to use relative goals and a percent-of-TIC (Target Incentive Compensation) approach. Using our New York and South Dakota reps as an example, under this method, they would each have a $20,000 annual target incentive, and when the New York rep reaches his goal of $2 million, and the South Dakota rep reaches her goal of $1 million, they would each be paid $20,000. The only thing that changes the amount paid is the percent of goal achieved: 90 percent of goal may pay only $10,000 (50 percent-of-TIC) while 110 percent of goal may pay $30,000 (150 percent-of-TIC). This is called a "Cost-of-Labor" approach and places more emphasis on the market value of the job and goal attainment than the pure economic relationship between volume sold and amount paid. With some signification exceptions, most sales forces in the United States use some form of Cost-of-Labor as their primary approach to managing pay. I find this combination can be the solution to what otherwise seem to be unsolvable compensation problems.

For those who are squeamish about going to the full Cost-of-Labor approach, there is a compromise. You can use relative goals but still pay for volume. You do this by setting a goal attainment scale that changes the commission rate. For example:

- 0–50 percent of goal: Commission rate is 5 percent
- 50–100 percent of goal: The rate becomes 10 percent
- 100 percent of goal: The rate is 15 percent

This allows the South Dakota rep to reach higher commission rates faster, but still recognizes that $2 million in sales is more than $1 million in sales and pays more for it. You can also do the opposite and use absolute goals, but pay using a percent-of-TIC approach as this allows you to more finely manage pay transitions between career levels without showing a commission rate. This is quite a common choice for many brokers. In any case, I always recommend using tiers or levels of expectation (at least three), as this allows for a finer degree of control over the cost of compensation at different performance levels as well as increasing the motivation for your team. You can raise tiers far more easily than you can decrease commission rates.

In the next chapter, we will tackle scope of measurement (individual, team, or company) and crediting point (shipment, delivery, release, invoice, payment, or some other point in time), which are concepts that are a bit easier to digest.

Chapter 12

Selecting Scope of Measure and Identifying the Ideal Crediting Point

In this chapter, we will deal with scope (level of aggregation) and crediting point ("When is a sale a sale?" or "When is a load a load?" for incentive compensation purposes).

Scope of measurement is about whose performance counts, and this is one of the fun points in a design discussion, because once managers realize they can have their cake and eat it too, they get really enthusiastic about continuing with the process. Many organizations struggle endlessly with the individual-versus-team tug-of-war. We addressed this in chapter 9, when we assigned weights to our measures and debated the need for a team load-count measure. To refresh your memory, we selected the following three performance measures and associated plan weights:

- **Element #1:** GP$ with GP% modifier: 50 percent

- **Element #2:** New carriers: 30 percent

- **Element #3:** Team load count: 20 percent

We've already agreed that Element #3's scope of measurement would be team-based, but which team are we talking about? Even small brokers often have two levels of team that could be considered when talking about load count: the operations team and then above that, the total company. In some cases, the total load count could be the same for both levels of aggregation, but in others the operations load-count number could be smaller than the total company number if some of the loads are covered by the sales team, or there are agents who handle their own loads, or there are dispatchers for contract carriers who are not part of the carrier sales operations team. Remember, the further you go away from the individual level in scope of measurement, the less control an individual employee

DETAILED DESIGN DECISIONS

- **TIC (Target Incentive Compensation) Anchor Point:** Fixed by role, or percent of salary or midpoint?

- **Goal Setting Approach:** Absolute (common for all) versus relative (unique by person or group)?

- **Payment Method:** Percent-of-volume, or percent-of-TIC?

- **Scope:** What level of aggregation is used in the measure (i.e., when we say team, what team?)?

- **Crediting Point:** When is a load a load for the plan: pickup, delivery, invoice, payment, or some other point that makes sense for your company?

- **Performance Period:** What time horizon do you want to use: monthly, quarterly, annually?

- **Pay Frequency:** How often do you want (or need) to make incentive payments? This is not the same thing as performance period, as you can use an annual goal, but make monthly payments against progress toward that goal.

- **Performance Ranges:** What constitutes minimal acceptable performance (threshold), target performance, and excellence?

- **Use of caps or decelerators:** Are they necessary? How good is your crystal ball?

- **Use of qualifiers, modifiers, kickers, depressors, and cross-gates:** What protections need to be in place?

has over the result, and the less motivational the incentive plan will be. At the most extreme end of the team spectrum are profit-sharing plans based on EBITDA or earnings-per-share. Most workers inside a company don't understand these calculations, are not given the information necessary to validate them, and don't perceive themselves as having any measurable impact on the results. At the other end, using a 100 percent individual plan, however, often leads to competitiveness, selfishness, and potentially even dishonesty if too much pay is a risk.

So, in our example, the company has a small operations team of thirteen carrier sales reps split into three pods. One pod has three reps, another has four reps, and another has six reps. The pods are organized by region based on freight origin. The pods are staffed according to the volume in the region. Teamwork is high within a pod, but reps rarely provide cross-pod support. Therefore, the design team decides that the scope for Element #3: load count should be at the pod level. If it were the case that they often provided cross-pod support, then I would likely push the team to consider using the sum of all three pods (the "operations team") as the scope of measurement, and if this number was identical to the company-load-count number, we might just call it "company load count" to make it easy to understand what is referenced.

That was pretty easy. Now, let's look at Element #1. It actually has two measures: gross profit dollars (GP$) and gross profit percentage (GP%). There is no rule that says both have to be the same scope. *What?* Yes! With a modifier, you can mix and match if it makes sense to do so. You could decide that you want GP$ goals to be set at the individual level, but GP% goals set at the pod level. This might help discourage one pod member from moving a load at a lower profit percentage just to get full credit when a teammate can get a better rate and boost the overall team percentage by doing so. Or there might be some rationale to flip it and set GP$ at the pod level and GP% at the individual level. It's really up to you how you want the team to work together. For this example, our team decides that Element #3 is sufficient for teamwork and wants to use an individual scope of measurement for both parts of Element #1.

Last but not least is Element #2: New carriers. At the moment, this is a bit of a black box. GP$, GP%, and team load-count are pretty straightforward as measures, but what are new carriers? Well, they are carriers that are new, but does this mean "new" because they have never moved a load, or only not in the last twelve months? Do they just have to be set up in the system as a potential carrier, or do they actually have to move a load? (This one should be obvious, as if you pay an incentive for having new carriers set up in your system, very quickly you will have a ton of new carriers—perhaps not much else). If you count one load as the qualification for a new carrier, the scope could be at the individual level, but what if you decide they need to move more than one load to count, because really what you are after are good new carriers with whom you can build a relationship? Uh-oh. Now we have a problem, because you will need five or ten or twenty loads for a carrier to qualify, and they are unlikely to have all been dispatched by the same carrier sales rep unless you are using an owned carrier system.[11] While you might *like* to use individual scope for this measure, in all likelihood you will need to have a team-based scope and credit all team members when a new carrier qualifies (or all team members who move at least one load on that carrier).

This measure is potentially messy, and will clearly need some more work. For now, we will just say that we know that it needs to be a team-based measure and, in fact, may need to be the entire operations team, as one carrier could operate in multiple geographies that cross over pods.

Our last topic for this chapter is credit point: When is a load a load for our carrier sales team? This has to do with the date in the system that is used to pull the incentive reports. The choices are usually, but not exhaustively:

- Shipment date

- Delivery date

- Release date

- Invoice date or bill date

- Payment date

- Accounting reconciliation (audit) date

Generally, the rule is that the closer the crediting point is to the actual sales event, the more motivational the plan will be. However, if you credit too close in, you run the risk of having to do lots of adjustments to account for TONUs (truck order not used), extra accessorial charges, or other issues. So the answer is to find the place along the spectrum where you are comfortable that adjustments will be rare exceptions, but as close to load shipment as possible.[12] A quick review of the plans we have developed for more than 100 brokers shows that *delivery date* is the most common selection, with *invoice date* as the second most common. Note that picking invoice date has the benefit of ensuring paperwork is completed accurately and in a timely manner. However, it also means that your accounting staff will be really stressed, as the carrier sales team will be pressuring them to process invoices as quickly as possible. This could be good or bad. You have to decide where you want to focus and what problems you are trying to solve. Many CFOs want to use payment date, but it will be difficult for the staff to anticipate how much they will be credited in a given period, as they do not control customer payment terms. It also tends to turn them into collection agents

---

[11] There is not enough space in this book to debate the merits of an owned carrier system, but generally I have seen few instances where it works well. Most typically clients tell us they tried it and then moved away from it quickly because it created more problems than it solved. There is one very large broker who has been successful using this method for a long time, but it is likely they have other supporting systems that make it more feasible for them than for smaller brokers.

[12] Except in cases of long-term contract sales that guarantee a certain number of loads, we've not seen a crediting point earlier than shipment (such as contract signing) used in a true brokerage.

and creates some problems for certain types of commission arrangements as you may find yourself establishing a commission rate for the month based on volume delivered during the month, but then you are either tracking that rate against each shipment and paying the commission as payment is received, or calculating the rate on loads delivered in the month and applying that rate to loads paid in the month (so the two gross profit amounts are not congruent—high volume of delivered loads may create a high commission rate but it gets applied to a low volume of "paid in" shipments). We've seen both, and there are significant complications and gaming potential with both. If you don't have a problem with accounts receivable (A/R), then it's probably not necessary to hold incentive calculations until payment is received. However, if your A/R is out of control, or if the role in question makes credit decisions, or if you've experienced significant levels of fraud by your staff[13], then you almost certainly should use payment as the crediting point. You need to know your situation and decide accordingly.

Note that you should *not* try to adjust for every penny that does not come through exactly the way you credited in the incentive plan. Incentive compensation is about motivating behavior, not creating an economically precise allocation of dollars between the company and the employee. If your employee has any kind of salary, you are already imprecise in the work delivered for the pay received, so why would you obsess over pennies in the incentive plan? You should have your employees working to get the next load covered, rather than spending time in accounting arguing over a few dollars.

Now that we have determined scope, we can decide how we want to handle goal-setting and payment method (it is difficult to have these discussions before you decide scope). Based on the psychological discussion we had in chapter 4 on the value of non-pay-related factors such as career progression, the team has decided to use three levels of carrier sales rep: Carrier Sales I, II, and III. Each level will have a different individual GP$ goal that represents the increasing skill and experience that justifies a promotion to the higher level. Within a level, however, every carrier sales rep will have the same GP$ goal. This is a combination of relative (between levels) and absolute (within level) goals that has worked well for many brokers. The team's initial thinking is that using a volume-based pay method (commission) would make the most sense and be the easiest for the team to understand in transition as they are on a straight commission currently.

The GP% metric will likewise be a combination of absolute and relative. There are three different pods that manage different geographies. Therefore, it would be unfair to hold them to the same GP% standard (we all know that freight out of California has a different GP%

[13] It would probably be better to deal with the staff members who are committing fraud through immediate termination rather than dampening the motivational value of your incentive plan by holding payment for everyone else. One or two quick terminations for this behavior usually puts an end to it. The typically two-to-four-week delay in processing incentive payments is usually sufficient to catch and correct bogus loads that have been entered before they are paid out. However, if you are paying very quickly after the end of the performance period or very frequently (such as every two weeks) then you may need to be more vigilant to catch fraud before it becomes an errant incentive payment issue.

than freight out of Florida). Therefore, the GP% targets will be aligned to the pod assignment (relative), but common for all reps within the pod (absolute). This will generate nine potential goal combinations for GP$ and GP%, as each pod could have all three levels of carrier sales rep represented.

Element #2, new carriers, is likely going to be at the pod or company level and could probably be set using an absolute goal as each pod should have a reasonably similar opportunity to add new carriers. The team believes that a percent-of-TIC pay method will be more sensible here than a volume-based method, but there could be other options (such as a bounty) to be determined later.

Element #3, team load count, we have determined is more properly called Pod Load Count, and will likely need to have relative goals as each pod will have a different freight mix they are dealing with based on geography, with differences in GP% and profit per load leading to pretty different load-count expectations. Therefore, each pod will need to have a different load-count goal. The team believes that a percent-of-TIC payment method makes more sense here than a volume-based method, as the goals will be set based on what is realistically possible for each pod's given freight mix. Volume doesn't matter as much as reaching the goal and the pay should be the same for each team that reaches goal, regardless of what the goal is.

In the next chapter, we will tackle performance period and pay frequency (which many think are the same thing, but they are not). There are a lot of unintended consequences that can be avoided by making the right choices for these two decision points.

Chapter 13

Performance Periods and Pay Frequencies: More Options Than You Can Imagine

This chapter will address the next two compensation design decision questions: performance period and pay frequency, which are misunderstood and commonly overlooked.

Companies often answer the second question (pay frequency) first, based on nothing more scientific than, "That is how we've always done it." For some, this means incentives are paid weekly and for others it means they are paid once per year (usually at the end of the year). In these cases, pay frequency is primarily a function of pay mix. 100-percent-variable plans must be paid more frequently (weekly, bi-weekly or monthly), as this is the only income for the employee. Incentive plans with very little pay at risk are often paid annually, as to do otherwise would make the payout too small to be meaningful. In general, the answer should be to pay as frequently as possible while not:

- Creating undue administrative burden (paying daily, while highly motivational, would be costly to administer)

- Making payouts too small to be meaningful (you want the employee to see a difference in his or her check from the incentive to drive behavior; the amount that is "too small" is relative, as someone who makes $150,000 a year will have a different perception of small than someone who makes $25,000 a year)

The more interesting question is performance period and how it relates to pay frequency. The performance period should relate to the business cycle and to the focal point management would like to create. As you may have gathered from this book already, there is rarely one right answer. In fact, it is often best for organizations to blend performance periods within a compensation plan. For example, our carrier sales sample role has three measures and weights:

DETAILED DESIGN DECISIONS

- **TIC (Target Incentive Compensation) Anchor Point:** Fixed by role, or percent of salary or midpoint?

- **Goal Setting Approach:** Absolute (common for all) versus relative (unique by person or group)?

- **Payment Method:** Percent-of-volume, or percent-of-TIC?

- **Scope:** What level of aggregation is used in the measure (i.e., when we say team, what team?)?

- **Crediting Point:** When is a load a load for the plan: pickup, delivery, invoice, payment, or some other point that makes sense for your company?

- **Performance Period:** What time horizon do you want to use: monthly, quarterly, annually?

- **Pay Frequency:** How often do you want (or need) to make incentive payments? This is not the same thing as performance period, as you can use an annual goal, but make monthly payments against progress toward that goal.

- **Performance Ranges:** What constitutes minimal acceptable performance (threshold), target performance, and excellence?

- **Use of caps or decelerators:** Are they necessary? How good is your crystal ball?

- **Use of qualifiers, modifiers, kickers, depressors, and cross-gates:** What protections need to be in place?

- **Element #1:** GP$ with GP% modifier: 50 percent
- **Element #2:** Team new carriers: 30 percent
- **Element #3:** Pod load count: 20 percent

We do not have to use the same performance period for all three elements. In fact, it probably would be a bad idea to do so, as then everyone would be focused on either a short-term horizon or a long-term horizon. The best approach for the organization is a balance of short- and long-term focus as you need short-term focus for urgency but you need long-term focus for organizational health.

Note also there is a subtle but important difference between performance period and pay frequency. Pay frequency describes how often incentive checks are cut and delivered to the staff. Performance period describes a time bucket that measures performance against some kind of goal or expectation across that time. These are not always the same.

We have seen the following performance periods selected by brokers:

- Weekly (common in quasi-agent models with no salary); in this case it may be that each load generates its own payout and there really is no aggregated performance period, just an accumulation of payout values for individual transactions. In one case a broker used a daily performance period[14] (with pay varying by daily production goal attainment) and paid the accumulated incentive at the end of the week.

- Bi-weekly (rare, but we have seen it when there is much pay at risk); this could also be a simple accumulation of transactional pay amounts paid out every two weeks, but it is possible (though rare) that goals and performance against goals could be assessed every two weeks or against a four week goal but paid on a period to date basis.

- Every four weeks (common in asset associated brokerages as this is often how "monthly" is measured for trucking companies, note: there are 13 of these periods in a year).

- (Calendar) Monthly (very common).

- (Calendar or fiscal) Quarterly (very common) or alternatively, every 13 weeks if using a four-week "monthly" period, or sometimes quarters are defined as two four-week months and one five-week month (this is referred to as "4-4-5," but the "5" could be in any position within the cycle).[15]

---

[14] We always recommend using some performance period as you cannot set goals and vary pay in any fashion around the goal (other than a straight line), without one.

[15] Our guidance here is to use whatever is currently in place for your accounting system. Do not use a different method for the incentive plan than what is used for business accounting, as it's unlikely accounting will want to (or should) change their methods to accommodate a new incentive approach.

- Semi-annually (rare except for 3PL/supply chain sales which can have a sales cycle measured in years).

- Annually (common for admin support roles or others tied only to an overall company performance number).

Please note that changing pay frequency can be difficult for your staff as it can affect their cash flow. If you are reducing the frequency of incentive payouts (such as going from weekly to monthly) you may need to set up a bridge plan for the first few months so your staff has time to shift the timing of their bills to correspond to the longer wait between payments (see chapter 19 for more details on bridge plans). If you are increasing frequency, there is usually not as much of an issue. Decreasing frequency may also increase the amount of taxes withheld from each check as it will create a larger single payment which may fall into a higher tax bracket. The staff will of course get any excess withholding back when they file taxes at year-end, but a change to a longer pay frequency may necessitate updating their W-4 withholding amounts.

Balance Performance Periods and Pay Frequency Using a True-Up

Our sample brokerage already measures most of their statistics on the basis of a calendar month, so it makes sense to continue to do so for the GP$ and GP%. Your carrier sales manager raises a red flag, however. Some months have fewer working days than other months, so she is concerned that when measured against a standard monthly goal, some months will be too easy and others too hard. The choices here are to "peg the middle" and use a wide enough performance range (see chapter 15) so as to dampen the negative or positive impact of changes in available working days, or to restate the goal as a daily average, which remains a constant number from month to month. The challenge with using a daily average number (or any average for that matter) is that toward the end of the month it becomes difficult to move the needle very much.

Your CFO is concerned about seasonality in that performance can swing widely from month to month, creating large payouts one month and small payouts the next if you are only using a "discrete monthly" performance period where each month starts fresh and stands alone without relation to what came before or what comes after. However, once you introduce goals or performance expectations into your plan, you now can employ the concept of a true-up. This allows for the smoothing of performance over a longer period while continuing to pay more frequently. The most common form of this approach is a discrete period, paid up to 100 percent of goal, followed by a true-up period that sums up the discrete periods, calculates payout for the longer true-up period, and subtracts the payments made for the shorter discrete periods. If performance is strong over the longer period, there will be an additional payout available to the employees in the form of a true-up.

The two most common true-up approaches are:

- Discrete monthly with a quarter-end true-up

- Discrete quarterly with a year-end true-up

A true-up approach also has the advantage of delaying payment for top performers until later in the year, providing a form of golden handcuffs in the compensation plan. Note that payouts are capped for the shorter period, typically at 100 percent of the goal. Then payouts at the true-up are allowed to run to the maximum possible payout.

We had a perfect example of the wisdom of using a true-up approach in the fall of 2012. We rolled out an uncapped discrete monthly plan for a broker with staff along the East Coast. The first month under the new plan was November, 2012. Hurricane Sandy hit, along with an avalanche of Federal Emergency Management Agency (FEMA) loads. One broker ended up at 800 percent of goal. Certainly he worked hard, but he didn't create the hurricane. If we had used a true-up approach, the payout would have still been very high for the quarter, but it would have smoothed out a bit when December and January freight volumes returned to normal.

Different Performance Period and Pay Frequency Options

For completeness, I need to mention the other performance periods that are possible. And for those who think that I'm making this stuff up, all of these are real examples from real clients we've worked with. Each approach has merit and can be the right answer for a given situation. It just depends on what your needs and goals are.

Note: *For each "Period" below you can insert the word monthly, quarterly, or annually to get a better idea how this works.*

- **Discrete Period** (e.g., discrete monthly): Each period stands alone and starts fresh. This is very common among freight brokers as it is very simple and generates a lot of urgency if used with short periods.

- **Period 1-to-Date with Period 2 True-Up** (e.g., year-to-date with quarterly true-up): Each period adds to the one prior and subtracts previous payments.

- **Period 1 Cumulative with Period 2 Progress Payments** (e.g., annual cumulative with quarterly progress payments): Periodic payments are made toward a long-term goal, such as paying quarterly against an annual goal. Q1 results should be tracking to 25 percent of the annual goal and are paid accordingly. This is very rare in brokerage, as it often delays payout until August or September, when the threshold of the annual goal is reached. However, we have seen it used for kickers, such as when a higher commission rate is earned once an overall annual productivity level is reached.

- **Discrete Period 1 with Accumulated Period 2 Payments** (e.g., discrete daily, with accumulated weekly payments): In this version the performance period is shorter than the pay period (the reverse of all the others which are either the same, or the pay period is shorter than the performance period). This is sometimes used for daily measurement of pay that is accumulated and paid out weekly or weekly measurement that is accumulated and paid out monthly. This approach can be problematic if you wait too long to make the payment, as it can start to feel like a holdback, which is illegal in some states. Typically, when you calculate an incentive and declare an amount "earned," payout should follow quickly with the only delay being processing time through payroll.

- **Rolling Period 1 with Payment Period 2 as Earned** (e.g., rolling twelve-month with payment quarterly as earned): This is commonly used for bounties or banks which track performance beyond a finite period and are waiting for events to happen before payment is earned. In this method, there may not be a payout every pay cycle (as the event to trigger a payout may not have happened), but in the next pay cycle several events may have happened creating a large payout. As such, this method can create very lumpy payments and is best used for secondary plan elements.

In our example, our team decides on the following method to balance performance period and pay frequency in their plan design:

- **Element #1:** Individual GP$ with individual GP% modifier: 50 percent—measured using a discrete monthly period and paid monthly (within 15-30 days following the close of the month)

- **Element #2:** Team new carriers: 30 percent—measured using a discrete-quarterly period and paid quarterly (within 15-30 days following the close of the quarter)

- **Element #3:** Pod load-count: 20 percent—paid using a discrete quarterly period with a cap of 100 percent followed by an annual true-up; payments will be quarterly with a 5th payment at year-end if the true-up calculation warrants it.

The next chapter will tackle performance ranges and the use (or nonuse) of caps or qualifiers, modifiers, kickers, depressors, and cross-gates.

Chapter 14

Keeping Things Under Control: Capping, Qualifying, Modifying, Kicking, Gating and Linking

This chapter will cover performance ranges, the use of caps, and various types of qualifiers and modifiers. First, let's review some terms we learned in chapter 7.

- **Threshold:** The minimum level of performance required to justify any incentive payout

- **Target/Goal/Quota:** The level that should be attainable by a fully-trained person in the role (expected performance)

- **Excellence:** A high level of attainment typically achieved by no more than the top 10 percent of the employee population within the role

We use these three inflection points to develop a plan that will continually push employees to higher levels of performance. Additional tiers may be added, but these are usually the only three needed to set up the framework and determine the payout curve between performance tiers. A good rule of thumb is to develop your plan so that you expect 50–60 percent of your employees to be at or above target performance, no more than 10 percent below threshold, and no more than 10 percent at or above excellence. This doesn't mean you should reverse-engineer the goals after the performance period is over to create a forced bell curve, but it does mean you should look at historical data carefully and make a highly educated guess.

When you gather your historical data, you need to do a little clean-up first:

- Address partial-year employees through exclusion or annualization (if you have a large enough employee

DETAILED DESIGN DECISIONS

- **TIC (Target Incentive Compensation) Anchor Point:** Fixed by role, or percent of salary or midpoint?

- **Goal Setting Approach:** Absolute (common for all) versus relative (unique by person or group)?

- **Payment Method:** Percent-of-volume, or percent-of-TIC?

- **Scope:** What level of aggregation is used in the measure (i.e., when we say team, what team?)?

- **Crediting Point:** When is a load a load for the plan: pickup, delivery, invoice, payment, or some other point that makes sense for your company?

- **Performance Period:** What time horizon do you want to use: monthly, quarterly, annually?

- **Pay Frequency:** How often do you want (or need) to make incentive payments? This is not the same thing as performance period, as you can use an annual goal, but make monthly payments against progress toward that goal.

- **Performance Ranges:** What constitutes minimal acceptable performance (threshold), target performance, and excellence?

- **Use of caps or decelerators:** Are they necessary? How good is your crystal ball?

- **Use of qualifiers, modifiers, kickers, depressors, and cross-gates:** What protections need to be in place?

population, exclusion is best, but if you have a small company you may need to annualize)

- Remove unusual sales or transactions that are not likely to be repeated

- Remove transactions that are not credited to the staff or are zero value transactions (e.g., TONU) as they can distort the data

- Consider other special circumstances that may be found in the data and adjust accordingly

Once your data are cleaned up, we need to get a sense of the range of historical performance for each metric we are using in the plan. To refresh, we are using:

- **Element #1:** Individual GP$ and Individual GP%—discrete monthly

- **Element #2:** Team new carriers—discrete quarterly

- **Element #3:** Pod load count—quarterly with annual true-up

The scope matters because it dictates the level of aggregation you will need, as do the performance periods and crediting points. Our team decided to use delivery date as the best crediting point to balance near-term motivation, ease in communication and calculation, and minimal post-payment adjustments. You will need to aggregate the data so it aligns with the scope and performance period, meaning in this case you will need to look at total GP$ and GP% by person by month (so twelve data points for each carrier sales rep); you will need to look at total new carriers for the entire company by quarter (four total data points); and total load count by pod by quarter (four data points for each pod). Once you have aggregated your transaction-level data, you can now begin your analysis, looking for 10th, 25th, 50th, 60th, 75th, and 90th percentiles (see Excel Tip sidebar for more info). You can do this one period at a time to get a sense of seasonal skew (e.g., June GP$ 50th percentile may be $40,000, whereas in January it's $25,000), or you can look at all months together (the overall annual median GP$ is $32,500). That will depend on how big a data set you have and whether you are considering setting variable goals by month or quarter (of course, if you have very large swings from period to period, you may have to adjust the goals throughout the year).

This analysis should give you a clear picture of what is possible and what is not possible for your staff. You should not set a goal or performance expectation that far exceeds the median of your historical data. Setting it a smidge above the median is fine; this will push performance up, and we like to use the 60th percentile to set this bar. But don't set goal at the 90th percentile, as this will be demoralizing. Set your threshold somewhere between the 10th and 25th percentiles and excellence around the 90th percentile, give or take, based on your confidence in the data.

Excel Tip

A pivot table is a fast way to aggregate transaction-level data, but I prefer to use Excel's Table feature to create my own summary sheet using SUMIFs and COUNTIFs. If you use a pivot table, be sure to add your own calculation for weighted GP% (Sum of GP$/Sum of Revenue $), as Excel's pivot feature will give you a SUM of the individual transaction GP% values, and AVERAGE just yields the simple average of each transaction's GP%. The syntax for the percentile function is =PERCENTILE(ARRAY,.10) to find the 10th percentile of an array of data, such as A1:A100. Be careful you do not have your data filtered, because PERCENTILE will include hidden cells in the calculation. It is far better to sort your data by role, team, division, or whatever grouping you need first, and then run your analysis.

Advanced tip: if you want to set up a separate tab to house your formulas and you don't want to have to change the ranges every time you add to the data, you can create the equivalent of PERCENTILEIF using an array feature something like this (but be sure to search for tips on entering array formulas in Excel, as you must enter the formula by using CONTROL+SHIFT+ENTER rather than just ENTER (this puts the { } around the formula—you cannot enter them manually)) {=PERCENTILE(IF((ROLE="Carrier Sales")*(MONTH="March"),GROSS_PROFIT),.90)} Substitute your title for "carrier sales" and be sure it is written in the formula exactly as it is in your data set. Note that ROLE, MONTH, and GROSS_PROFIT are all named ranges indicating the array in the data set. Named ranges are very handy for keeping track of what your formulas are trying to accomplish, but you will need to actually name the ranges with these names to make this formula work.

Another mathematical rule for incentive plan design is the Law of Large Numbers. This means that while you may see wide swings in performance at the individual level, as you aggregate employees into teams, divisions, groups, etc., the swings will become much shallower as the highs and lows balance each other out. The practical result of this is managers (whose goals are a team aggregation) have narrower performance ranges in their plans than individual employees (for more on this see chapter 18).

Next comes the question of caps. We prefer to avoid caps for any measure that directly relates to revenue or profit and is controlled by the individual, unless there is some reason to turn off sales. Note, however, that team-based incentives are almost always capped. This ensures that the deadweight member of the team (and every team has one) is not disproportionately rewarded by a big team payout. If for some reason you have an exclusively team-based plan, you might uncap it with a regressed payout curve, but include a strong individual performance modifier or cross-gate to ensure the money is going to the right people.

So the team decides to uncap GP$, but there is a natural cap on the GP% element (could anyone actually achieve 100 percent GP% in a month? Not unless they own a truck and are moving your freight themselves for free). So often companies will set a narrower range of performance around GP% (10 percent to 20 percent, with 15 percent as the center, is quite common these days), and leave the GP$ element to run unlimited. We often recommend regressing the payout curve above excellence, however, for an uncapped plan. This means that if the rate of pay is going up 3× for every 1× in performance, then above excellence, we would want the rate pay to go up 1.5× for every 1× in performance. This provides some protection against windfalls, bluebirds, and hurricanes that create a deluge of FEMA loads.

Fine-Tuning the Results: Qualifiers, Modifiers, Kickers, Depressors, and Cross-Gates

OK, so an uncapped plan on GP$ is all well and good, but what if the person's average GP% is 5 percent for the month? Do we still want to pay them the same as someone whose average was 20 percent? Probably not. Yes, a dollar is a dollar, but the 5-percent person is straining your systems with a high volume of low-value freight, and the 20-percent person is probably doing a far better job negotiating. So here are some options:

- Use GP% as a qualifier: e.g., "Your GP% must be above 10 percent to earn any payout under Element #1". This is an on/off switch.

- Use GP% as a modifier: e.g., this simple, three-tiered approach:

    - GP% < 10.00 percent = 80 percent modifier (20 percent of the payout under the GP$ calculation is forfeited)

    - GP% 10.00–15.00 percent = 100 percent modifier (no change to GP$ calculated payout)

    - GP% 15.01 percent and up = 120 percent modifier (GP$ calculation gets an extra 20 percent)

- Use GP% as a kicker—only the 120 percent upside from the modifier applies.

- Use GP% as a depressor—only the 80 percent reduction from the modifier applies (I don't generally like depressors, as they are...depressing).

The cross-gate is a bit of a different idea, and is typically used for reps selling multiple product lines or individuals paid under both an individual- and team-based element. For our plan design, we could add a cross-gate that said: "Threshold level of performance must be attained on Element #1 (Individual GP$) for payout to be attained on Element #3 (Pod load count)." You can set a gate that eliminates payout altogether or limits payout on Element #3 to no more than 100 percent; it's up to you. A cross-gate tied to an individual element is an excellent way to ensure deadweight team members are not collecting large dollars from an otherwise outstanding team.

SECTION IV

Taming and Training Your Beast

Chapter 15

Incentive Compensation Mechanics

So, we've checked off all the detailed design decisions you need to make, and you probably thought you were done with your new compensation plan.

Far from it.

Now the real fun begins: we get to develop the specific pay mechanics—these are the actual mathematical formulas that will be used to determine payouts. The options are nearly endless.

But, before we get into that, let's recap where we landed on a variety of important decisions for our hypothetical carrier sales role. We have identified three elements, with the following design characteristics:

- **Target Total Compensation (TTC):** $48,000

- **Pay Mix:** 75/25

- **Base Salary Midpoint:** $36,000 ($28k min/$43k max, a 20 percent range around the midpoint)

- **Target Incentive:** $12,000

- **Leverage:** 3×, which means,

  - Excellence incentive of $36,000

  - Excellence total cash of $72,000 ($36k salary plus $36k excellence incentive)

(See chapter 9 for the discussion that led to the above decisions.)

Table 15.1: *Example Compensation Plan*

Design Decision	Element #1: GP$ and GP%	Element #2: Team New Carriers	Element #3: Pod Load Count
Weight	50 percent	30 percent	20 percent
Annual Target Incentive	$6,000 (50% of $12,000)	$3,600 (30% of $12,000)	$2,400 (20% of $12,000)
TIC Anchor Point	Fixed by role and level	Fixed by role and level	Fixed by role and level
Goal Setting Approach	Relative by level on GP$, relative by pod on GP%	Absolute	Relative by pod
Payment Method	Percent-of-volume	Percent-of-TIC	Percent-of-TIC
Scope	Individual	Company	Pod
Crediting Point	Delivery	Delivery	Delivery
Performance Period	Discrete monthly	Discrete quarterly	Quarterly with annual true-up
Pay Frequency	Monthly	Quarterly	Quarterly + Year-end
Target Incentive by Pay Period	$500 ($6,000/12 monthly payments)	$900 ($3,600/4 quarterly payments)	$600 ($2,400/4 quarterly payments)
Performance Ranges	TBD	TBD	TBD
Modifiers/Cross Gates	GP% modifies GP$	None	Consider cross-gate with E1 at threshold level
Caps?	Uncapped on GP$; Practical cap on GP%	Capped	Capped

OK, good. We've made a lot of decisions. But you have no idea (yet) how anything is going to be calculated. What performance will be required to get to the target incentive? What's the *math* behind all this? This phase of the work is called "mechanics development" because you actually need to develop the gears and levers that will make the machine crank out the payments to your staff (and profits to your bottom line). For this chapter and the next one, we are only going to deal with Element #1 (Elements #2 and #3 will be covered in chapters 17 and 18, as they each have their own complexities).

We already know a number of key things about the shape of the gearbox for Element #1. GP$ is uncapped, but GP% has a natural cap of 100 percent and a practical cap of around 25 percent. We want GP$ performance to be primary, with GP% a secondary modifier. So, let's tackle the bits we don't know yet. If you recall chapter 11, you will remember these two questions: (1) the way performance will be measured—absolute or relative goals, and (2) the form the payout will take—commission or percent of target incentive. Each payout option can be combined with each performance option giving us four possible combinations, but some combinations are more common than others.

Table 15.2: *Element #1 Payout Options*

Performance Options	Pay Options Percent-of-Volume (Commission)	Percent of TIC
Absolute (Fixed) Goals	Highly-Common Pair	Common Pair
Relative Goals	Uncommon Pair	Highly-Common Pair

For carrier sales, it is quite common to use Absolute (Fixed) Goals because there is enough consistency in freight availability that every rep with a similar experience level should be able to reach a common performance expectation. You may have different absolute goals if you have different types of carrier sales for different types of freight (e.g., Less Than Truckload [LTL], Heavy Haul or Over-Dimensional [HH/OD], or Temperature Controlled [TC]), but within a group of carrier sales reps, operating with the same level of experience and dealing with the same type of freight, the performance expectation likely will be the same.

The next decision, how you pay, can make or break the success of your compensation plan. But there is a pretty good cheater way to be sure you are not going to step in a big pile of resentment and resistance when you roll out the new plan. If you are currently using a true commission (percent-of-volume) approach and people have been getting paid significant amounts regularly, then you probably need to stick with that. If you have no incentive plan in place now, or your carrier sales reps have not really been paid much under the old plan, then you can move to the percent-of-TIC approach. Note that percent-of-TIC is the recommended option *if you can get there*. The challenge with using a percent-of-volume payouts (a true commission) is they are very addicting and very hard to retract. You can do it, but it takes time, and if you have a straight-commission plan now that is paying a percent of GP$, you probably have enough change management on your hands by adding GP% as a modifier and tiers to performance on the GP$ (not to mention Elements 2 and 3) that I would not recommend tackling the change from commission to percent-of-TIC approach right now. Part of being able to implement a successful compensation plan is knowing how much change your people can handle. The perfect plan means nothing if it is completely rejected by the staff. It is better to have a more-or-less "OK" plan that moves the needle in some critical areas and that is fully accepted by the staff. You can then work to improve the plan over the next couple of years.

In our example, we are going to assume this group of carrier sales reps' old plan paid a 10 percent commission on GP$ and management expected $10,000[16] per month in GP$. Furthermore, their old plan had a threshold of $5,000 that ensured they were covering their $3,000 per month base salary (with some allowance for benefits, etc.), but after the threshold was met, the plan was retroactive to dollar one (so at $5,000 the rep earned $500). Top performers rarely did more than $15,000 per month. Note that the old plan (conveniently) would pay an on-target performer $12,000 per year (10 percent × $10,000 × 12). So the good news is, we are not changing the expected payout amount—just what they have to do to get there.

I wish that every client worked out this neatly, but it's nearly a guarantee that your old plan will not map so cleanly to the new plan outline, and some finagling will be needed after you see the modeling results.

So, a simple first step to improve the mechanics is to use a retroactive tiered-commission structure with a third and fourth layer, as follows:

Table 15.3: *Retroactive Tiered-Commission Structure*

Monthly Performance	Retroactive Commission Rate	Amount Paid at Bottom of Tier	Amount Paid at Top of Tier
$0–$4,999	0 percent	$0	$0
$5,000–$9,999	5.0 percent	$250	$500 (rounded)
$10,000–$14,999	7.5 percent	$750	$1,125 (rounded)
$15,000 and up	10.0 percent	$1,500	Uncapped

Note that the first two layers are the same as the old plan, except the new rate needs to be half of the old rate. Why? This element is now only 50 percent of the plan. If you kept the 10 percent old rate and then added Elements 2 and 3, you would be overpaying everyone's target incentive by $6,000 per year. This will be an issue that needs to be repeatedly clarified for your staff during rollout, as they will fixate on the rate dropping from 10 percent to 5 percent.

In addition to the bad optics of the rate being cut in half, there are strange things that happen with retroactive commissions. The payout for the one extra dollar is disproportionate

---

[16] This is an example number only and does not mean you should expect $10,000 from your carrier reps. I'm using $10,000 because it is a round number that makes it easier to do some of the math in the examples. I have worked with companies that have expected half of this number, and others that have expected multiples of this number. It all depends on your type of freight, your systems, and your people.

to the value gained by the company, and the motivation to cheat to get that extra dollar of production is high. If you have this kind of plan in place, check the parking lot on smoking breaks; I'd be willing to bet your carrier sales reps will be out there buying and selling loads from each other.

As we discussed in chapter 3, a better approach is to use a marginal rate, which in this case has the added advantage of improving the optics on the rate.

Table 15.4: *Example Marginal Rate Table*

Monthly Performance	Marginal Commission Rate	Amount Paid at Bottom of Tier	Amount Paid at Top of Tier
$0–$4,999	0 percent	$0	$0
$5,000–$9,999	10.0 percent	$0	$500 (rounded)
$10,000–$14,999	12.5 percent	$500	$1,125 (rounded)
$15,000 and up	15.0 percent	$1,125	Uncapped

In this example, the rate is only applied to the dollars within the tier, so the 10 percent commission rate only applies to the $5,000 that falls between $5,000 and $10,000. For the third tier, the 12.5 percent commission rate applies only to the $5,000 between $10,000 and $15,000 and is added to the $500 earned at the top of the preceding tier.

You can scale this plan so that it pays far more at the higher levels of performance than the old 10 percent flat-rate plan did and management will be happy to pay it because those dollars are only going to top performers for top production. At $25,000 in production, the marginal commission plan above would pay $2,625 (15 percent × $10k) + (12.5 percent × $5k) + (10 percent × $5k), which is 10.5 percent of total production (this is called the "effective rate"). Both the retroactive plan and the old flat-rate plan would only pay $2,500 (10 percent). Plus, you get some serious motivational kick from being able to show a 15 percent rate where one never existed before. For a graphical look at the difference between marginal rates and retroactive rates, refer to Figure 3.1.

In the next chapter, we will look at the GP% modifier and different ways it can be applied to the marginal commission rate, as well as some other approaches for calculating a two-measure element, such as matrices, which are very popular among our clients.

Chapter 16

Modifiers and Matrices: Two May be Better than One

In the last chapter, we reviewed different options for calculating a commission payout on GP$ for our carrier sales role. Remember, when I use the word "commission," I mean only that we are calculating the incentive payout using a volume-based method that pays a percent of a dollar amount (in this case GP$). I use the word "incentive" to signify any and all money paid to an employee that is variable, based on performance, and not delivered in the form of fixed hourly or salary payment. There are lots of ways to pay incentives, and a commission mechanic is only one of them.

Now we will look at our secondary element, GP%, and the ways we can use it to modify the payment for GP$. This raises some interesting philosophical questions you will need to address with your leadership team, as $10,000 in GP$ at 5 percent and $10,000 in GP$ at 25 percent, is *still* $10,000. The lower the GP%, the more revenue and load volume required to generate the $10,000: at 10 percent, you needed $100,000 in revenue and if your average profit per load (PPL) is $150, this means you needed to move 67 loads. If your profit is 25 percent, then the revenue required to generate $10,000 in GP$ is $40,000, your profit per load is $375, and your load count is 27. Considered another way, at the higher GP% you only needed to do 40 percent of the work to make the same amount of money.

Before you say it should be obvious which is better, there *are* circumstances where the high volume/low profit play is the proper business strategy, such as positioning your company for sale (high revenue figures may help with valuation multiples); when you are breaking into a new market and need to gain share (price low to win the business and then prove good service over time to justify price increases); and other perfectly valid reasons. Most of our clients, though, would prefer 25 percent GP% over 10 percent GP% and are willing to pay more for it, because they recognize the operational cost-savings from having to deal with fewer loads.

So the easy way to think about how to create the dynamic between GP$ and GP% is to consider what you set as target GP% (at the time of publication, it was around 15 percent for dry van loads), what you consider to be minimal acceptable performance (maybe 10 percent), and what you would consider to be excellent performance (maybe 22 percent). Note that I'm not referring to the GP% of one particular load, but an overall monthly average. This is an important point, as many organizations calculate a commission on a per-load basis and may vary the commission rate based on the GP% of a load. While most TMS commission-calculation systems are set up this way (hint: it's easiest to program) I've rarely found it does much from a motivational perspective. Each load is pretty much worth exactly the same as the last; someone who does 150 percent of the volume of the average performer will make 150 percent of the pay (when it really should be more like 300 percent to get true motivation and reward actual effort), and differentiating the rate based on the profit of single loads leads to incredibly short-sighted behavior. Negative or low-value loads are shunned, when in fact they may be needed to deepen a customer's loyalty and decrease their price sensitivity. Owners may have this mentality, but your average front-line worker in a brokerage rarely will. By aggregating the volume and considering monthly or quarterly trends, you help your staff learn to think more about the long-term. You can reward them for doing the right thing for the long-term, rather than just for that single load.

Returning to the GP% modifier, if you have a sense of threshold, target and excellence, then you can assign a value to add or subtract from the initial payout. Let's assume a rep earned exactly $1,000 for the month on his or her GP$ commission. If his or her GP% was < 10 percent, you might want to only pay 80 percent or $800. If the GP% was > 22 percent, you might be willing to pay 120 percent, or $1,200. You can set values between these two extremes that pay 85 percent, 90 percent, 95 percent, 105 percent, 110 percent, 115 percent, etc. Note that at target (say, 15 percent GP%) the modifier value is 100 percent—it neither adds nor subtracts from the earned value. You would scale this based on the value to the business of the change in GP%.

Once you are headed down the path of a multi-tiered modifier, it may make sense to consider a matrix, which may look like this:

Figure 16.1: *Example Commission Rate Matrix*

	Commission Rate										
$15,000	4.00%	4.40%	4.80%	5.20%	5.60%	6.00%	6.80%	7.60%	8.40%	9.20%	10.00%
$13,750 - $14,999	3.75%	4.15%	4.55%	4.95%	5.35%	5.75%	6.42%	7.08%	7.75%	8.42%	9.08%
$12,500 - $13,749	3.50%	3.90%	4.30%	4.70%	5.10%	5.50%	6.03%	6.57%	7.10%	7.63%	8.17%
$11,250 - $12,499	3.25%	3.65%	4.05%	4.45%	4.85%	5.25%	5.65%	6.05%	6.45%	6.85%	7.25%
$10,000 - $11,249	3.00%	3.40%	3.80%	4.20%	4.60%	5.00%	5.27%	5.53%	5.80%	6.07%	6.33%
$8,750 - $9,999	2.88%	3.21%	3.54%	3.88%	4.21%	4.54%	4.81%	5.08%	5.34%	5.61%	5.88%
$7,500 - $8,749	2.75%	3.02%	3.28%	3.55%	3.82%	4.08%	4.35%	4.62%	4.88%	5.15%	5.42%
$6,250 - $7,499	2.63%	2.83%	3.03%	3.23%	3.43%	3.63%	3.89%	4.16%	4.43%	4.69%	4.96%
$5,000 - $6,249	2.50%	2.63%	2.77%	2.90%	3.03%	3.17%	3.43%	3.70%	3.97%	4.23%	4.50%
	10.00%-10.99%	11.00%-11.99%	12.00%-12.99%	13.00%-13.99%	14.00%-14.99%	15.00%-16.39%	16.40%-17.79%	17.80%-19.19%	19.20%-20.59%	20.60%-21.99%	>22%

Monthly GP$ (left vertical axis label)

Monthly GP% (bottom axis label)

This approach creates more balance between GP$ and GP%, as one is not so clearly secondary to the other, and the matrix gives you a finer degree of control over the relationship between them. In this example, the upper left and lower right corners are calibrated to pay a slightly higher rate for higher GP% on lower dollars. You may believe the exact opposite is the right approach, and that is fine. You can adjust the payout values in the corners to suit your philosophy and needs.

Astute readers will note that a matrix functions as retroactive commission, which I cautioned against in an earlier chapter. You are correct, generally speaking, a matrix is phrased so that in the example above, once you reach $5,000 and 10 percent in GP%, you get 2.5 percent back to the first dollar (though you could bake in a clause that says the rate is paid "on all dollars above a threshold value," such as $5,000; this would also have the effect of allowing you to show higher rates inside the table as you are paying the rate against fewer dollars to get the target payout). I'm not sure I could wrap my head around a way to make this into a marginal rate (let alone try to explain it), but I have found that the increased number of steps and the influence of the second dimension mitigate the risk of gaming caused by the stair-step function of retroactive rates. A matrix by its very nature forces employees to grapple with daily tradeoffs and consider the bigger picture rather than to focus in on the value of a single load.

Note that matrices are highly pliable. You can use them with absolute or relative goal-based plans (or a mixture) and you can use individual scope for one axis and team or company scope for the other axis. You can even calculate the payout as percent-of-volume (commission) or percent-of-TIC (just replace the commission rates inside the cells with values like 25%, 75%, 100%, 150%, etc.), and calculate the percentage against the monthly target incentive amount, or even using a fixed-dollar payout. Many brokerage clients prefer to show a fixed-dollar payout (in this case the value $500 would be at the very center of the table) as it reduces the amount of math the staff have to do to calculate their own payouts. Be aware, however, that a commission approach inside a matrix has a different dynamic within a cell than either a percent-of-TIC or fixed dollar payout. Under a commission, every additional GP$ provides a little additional income, because the commission rate in the cell is applied to all dollars. Under a percent-of-TIC or fixed-dollar payout, you have to get to the next cell up or over or up and over to get a higher payout: one more GP$ may have no effect.[17]

In chapters 17 and 18, we will look at bounties as well as tiered and linear incentives, as likely mechanical options for Elements 2 and 3.

---

[17] I have had clients also develop a 3-dimensional approach for a matrix by adding a modifier (e.g., GP$ and load count on the matrix with GP% modifier table beside it). Or, for the truly creative, they have used revenue and load count to determine the commission rate inside the matrix, and this rate is then applied to the GP$ generated during the period. Be careful getting too wild and crazy, however, as you will have to explain it and calculate it and employees don't trust compensation plans that they don't understand or that have too many moving parts.

Chapter 17

To Bounty or Not to Bounty—That is the Question

In this chapter, we will talk about two approaches for calculating the pay for Element #2—Team new carriers. As a brief reminder, we have set an annual target incentive of $3,600 for the Team new carriers element and decided to pay it quarterly.

Option #1: The Bounty

For new carriers, we could pay a bounty to the entire team when a new carrier ships its *Nth* load. I didn't define what *N* needs to be; each company is different. For some, one load shipped may be enough to say, "we have a new carrier!" while for others, it may need to be 100 loads. This is another place where your plan needs to be customized to your business objectives and strategy.

You also need to consider the amount you want to pay for each occurrence. Note that the annual target incentive is $3,600 *per person*, so if you have five carrier sales reps, you will be paying out $18,000 ($3,600 × 5) for new carriers to be acquired. I doubt you are going to want to pay $100 to each carrier sales rep (total $500) for the completion of *one* load. (I know a story about buying watermelons for $1 and selling them for $0.75 that would fall into this same category.) So, consider the total amount you will be paying out and how many loads will be needed to cover that payout by at least 3×[18].

A related question is: "How many new carriers do you need to add this year?" Let's make our math easy and say you need to add 100 carriers that deliver at least ten loads during the year. If you make $200 in GP$ per load, you will be moving $2,000 in GP on each new carrier: $200,000 in total. At the highest level, the math works pretty well if you have a staff of 5 carrier sales reps. In this case, you are paying a "bounty" of 9 percent ($18,000/$200,000). Our experience shows that at least 50 percent of new customers or new carriers gained through the bounty process go on to provide additional benefits that drop to the bottom line. Remember, however, that you also need to consider others who are being paid on the same GP$ and other places it is being credited (in this case, GP$ from loads moved on new carriers are also counted toward Element #1 for one of the carrier sales reps, and very likely for at least one shipper sales rep as well). So, make it worth your while—but also worth it for the rep. If you are paying $1 per new carrier, you aren't likely to get anyone's attention.

---

[18] There is no particular magic to the 3x ROI that I typically expect. You could go with slightly more or slightly less; it's up to you. We've just found that paying out 1/3 of the value of a single load for a one-time payout provides a nice kick to get attention and drive motivation while still providing economic value to the company.

Think about it this way. You have decided you want 100 new carriers and they have to deliver ten loads (within a reasonable time from the first load—let's say six months) to "count" for the bounty. This means your bounty payout would be $36 to each carrier sales rep per qualified carrier ($3,600 annual TIC/100 expected qualified carriers). You would be paying out $180 ($36 × 5) in total for $2,000 in GP$ moved on a new carrier. This "works" from both perspectives. Nine percent is probably OK for you (for the benefit of improving your good carrier base), and $36 is not a fortune for employees (but twenty-five of those per quarter is another $900 gross pay in their check).

You may be wondering why each team member gets the bounty. If you happen to run an owned-carrier operation, you may not need to do this, but many organizations allow carriers to be used by the entire carrier sales team. In this world, you don't want to try to figure out who moved the tenth load, or dividing the bounty among the three to four reps who moved loads on that carrier. It is far easier to just pay everyone and assume it will come out in the wash. Remember, incentive plans do not replace management. If you have deadweight on your team, management should deal with it—not the incentive plan.

Bounty Notes: For any bounty, you need to define a time limit from the first load so you are not tracking forever, and you also need to define what constitutes "new." A good rule for "new" is that the carrier (or customer) has not delivered (or shipped) a load in the last twelve months. This covers most seasonality fluctuations in which a carrier (or customer) may simply be dormant or busy doing other things. Bounties are also somewhat difficult to track, they usually run from one year to the next, and are paid as earned in the next pay cycle, so consider your administrative resources. Bounties can be good motivational tools, but they are a good bit of work on the backend.

Option #2: A Tiered Incentive

In this approach, you set a tiered goal and correlate payout to relative attainment of the goal. This is pretty simple to do and could look something like this:

Table 17.1: *Tiered Incentive Payout Table*

# of Qualified New Carriers per Quarter	Quarterly Incentive Paid	Percent-of-TIC Paid
0–9	$0	0%
10–14	$225	25%
15–19	$450	50%
20–24	$675	75%
25–29	$900	100%
30–34	$1,125	125%
35–39	$1,350	150%
40–44	$1,575	175%
45+	$1,800	200%

Note the performance is bucketed, inasmuch as there is nothing additional paid for the twenty-sixth, twenty-seventh, twenty-eighth, or twenty-ninth carrier. Thirty carriers must qualify to get the next level of payout. This is a bit like a retroactive commission and has some of the same risks, such as selling a load at a very low rate to a new carrier just to get them to be the thirtieth to qualify. Protections will need to be put in place to keep this from happening (e.g., loads must be >= $150 GP$ to count toward qualification).

Either the bounty or the tiered incentive approach will work, but the tiered incentive approach will be a bit more difficult as the team needs to get a certain number of carriers to qualify within the quarter for the payout. Under the bounty, they earn the incentive whenever the qualification event happens for each carrier. Also, under the bounty, there will be an additional incentive for the twenty-sixth, twenty-seventh, twenty-eighth, etc. carriers. However, the tiered incentive approach provides for protection against some new carriers not being terribly valuable. When you pay $180 for each one ($36 x 5 reps), you hope they all become valuable. When you pay $1,125 for fourteen new carriers ($225 x 5 reps) you are only paying $16 per carrier so you have a bit more wiggle room if you lose a few of them. Note that the tiered approach also allows for a threshold, in the example above there is nothing paid if only nine new carriers are added. Under the bounty approach, you are typically paying for the first one. The proper selection between the two options depends on what you are trying to accomplish. For our purposes in this example, we will assume the team selects the tiered incentive table with percentage of TIC as payout value.

Chapter 18

Linear Incentives—The Bedrock of Solid Plan Designs

So far, we've looked at commissions, matrices, bounties, and tiered incentives. I've saved the most common plan design mechanic for last. For anyone who has ever worked under a corporate bonus plan, this should look familiar to you. It's called a linear incentive because—well, it creates a line.

Generally, a linear mechanic is used witih a goal-based incentive, paying a fixed-dollar or percent-of-salary payout (as opposed to commissions which pay a percent-of-volume). We showed you how you can combine goals and commissions in chapter 11, and certainly this method creates lines also (recall from Figure 3.1 the different lines drawn when using a retroactive commission—it looks like stairs, a straight commission—straight line up from bottom left corner of grid to upper right corner of grid, and a marginal commission—a nice curve that drives more pay to the top performers, with less pay to the bottom performers). A linear incentive works a lot like a marginal commission, but it gives you even more control over the goals and the outcomes than a commission does, because you are setting both the goal and the payout and controlling the mathematical relationship between them at every point along the way, now and in the future.

The most common (and incorrect) form goes something like this: at 80 percent of goal, the employee is paid 80 percent of the target incentive; at 100 percent of goal he or she is paid 100 percent of the target incentive; and at 120 percent of goal, he or she is paid 120 percent of the target incentive. Not only is this boring, it overpays underperformers and underpays overperformers. For most organizations, 80 percent of goal attainment likely represents shrinkage over the prior year; if the growth goal is anything less than 25 percent, you are going backward to only reach 80 percent of the new goal:

- **Last year's results:** $1,000,000
- **25 percent growth goal:** $1,250,000
- **80 percent of new goal:** $1,000,000

If your growth goal is only 10 percent, then the new goal is $1,100,000 and, 80 percent of that is $880,000, or a loss of $120,000. Are you really going to pay someone 80 percent of their incentive for going backward? I thought not.

For this reason, you are more likely to want to pay perhaps 25 percent of the target incentive (or maybe you set the threshold at 90 percent of goal and pay 25 percent of the target incentive there; then at 100 percent of goal, you would certainly pay 100 percent of the incentive).

When we get above goal, a different question comes into play. If we take our first example, someone who exceeded the $1,250,000 by 20 percent achieved $1,500,000, or 50 percent growth over prior year. This seems like an achievement worth more than 20 percent additional incentive pay.

For the upper end of performance, in order to figure out the right inflection point and amount of pay at that point, you need to look at two things:

First, determine the performance attained by your 90th percentile rep (top 10 percent). Use a bit of Excel magic to figure this out. Look at your column of results that shows percent-of-goal attained and use *=percentile(Array,.90)* where array = the column that has all the percent-of-goal results. This will give you the percent-of-goal attained by your 90th-percentile performer (the person who is number ten in the list of 100, ranked highest to lowest). This is a good place to set the inflection point. Let's say our analysis revealed this is 120 percent of goal.

Second, look at your pay mix (we discussed pay mix in chapter 5). The more pay at risk, the more upside you should have for those who do well under the plan. If you are using an 80/20 or 75/25 pay mix, 2× upside is probably fine. If the plan is more variable (more pay at risk) than 75/25, you probably should use 2.5× or even 3× leverage. When you get in the zone of 60/40 or 50/50, you certainly should be using 3× leverage. Let's say for this plan we are using 2× leverage (200 percent of target incentive).

Now we put 1 and 2 together and we know that at 120 percent of goal we should be paying 200 percent of the target incentive. We now have the three key points we need to define the slope of our payout curve. (I know, I know—it's not really a curve—it's a series of lines, but that's what it's called, and be glad because if it really were a curve we'd need calculus rather than just linear algebra!)

At 80 percent of goal, we pay 25 percent of the target incentive. At 100 percent of goal, we pay 100 percent of target incentive. And at 120 percent of goal we pay 200 percent of the target incentive. Now, go way back in your memory to high school algebra. You are going to use $y = mx + b$, or the slope of the line formula, but don't freak out. It's not nearly as scary as it sounds, and all you really need to know is "change in y over change in x" to calculate the slope of the line. The x-axis is performance, and the y-axis is pay (remember, the y axis is the dependent variable—in the math, pay changes as a result of performance, which then sets up a circle in the psychology as higher pay should also reinforce and drive higher performance, which of course drives higher pay, etc.). So let's figure the slope of the first part of the line. Change in y (100 percent of pay minus 25 percent of pay) over change in x (100 percent of goal minus 80 percent of goal):

(100−25)/(100−80)

75/20 = 3.75

This means for every 1 percent of goal earned between 80 percent of goal and 100 percent of goal, an additional 3.75 percent of the target incentive is earned. So at 81 percent of goal, the payout is 25 percent + 3.75 percent, or 28.375 percent. This continues to 100 percent.

Now, at 100 percent, something happens. The slope of the line changes. We now have change in y (200 percent of target incentive minus 100 percent of target incentive) over change in x (120 percent of goal minus 100 percent of goal).

(200−100)/(120−100)

100/20 = 5

This means for every 1 percent of goal above 100 percent, an additional 5 percent of target incentive is earned. So 101 percent of goal pays 100 percent + 5 percent, or 105 percent, 102 percent of goal pays 110 percent, etc., all the way to 120 percent of goal. The example below shows how the lines would look if you had set performance range at 50 percent to 150 percent and paid 25 percent at threshold (50 percent of goal) and 250 percent at excellence (150 percent of goal). Check the math and see if you can use different inflection points and payout values to derive different slopes.

Figure 18.1: *Example Payout Slope*

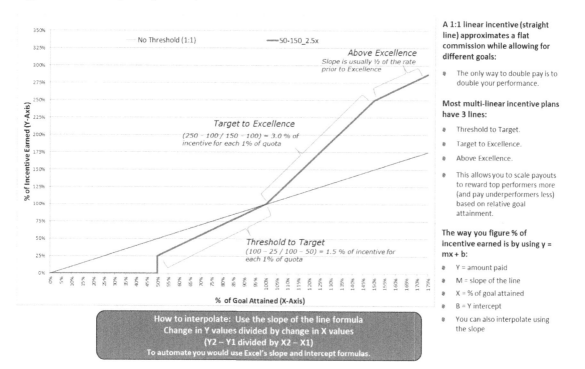

To make it easier to communicate to your staff, we often use a table like this to help them easily understand how to calculate their payout based on the percent of goal attained:

Figure 18.2: *Example Linear Incentive Staff Communication Table*

% of Goal	% of Target Incentive	% of Goal	% of Target Incentive
79%	0.00%	100%	100.00%
80%	25.00%	101%	105.00%
81%	28.75%	102%	110.00%
82%	32.50%	103%	115.00%
83%	36.25%	104%	120.00%
84%	40.00%	105%	125.00%
85%	43.75%	106%	130.00%
86%	47.50%	107%	135.00%
87%	51.25%	108%	140.00%
88%	55.00%	109%	145.00%
89%	58.75%	110%	150.00%
90%	62.50%	111%	155.00%
91%	66.25%	112%	160.00%
92%	70.00%	113%	165.00%
93%	73.75%	114%	170.00%
94%	77.50%	115%	175.00%
95%	81.25%	116%	180.00%
96%	85.00%	117%	185.00%
97%	88.75%	118%	190.00%
98%	92.50%	119%	195.00%
99%	96.25%	120%	200.00%

For each % above 120.00%, add 2.50% of your Target Incentive. For Example 122.00% of Goal = 205.00% of your Target Incentive

OK, so now you understand *how* it works, but what about *why*? When would you use a wide performance range (50-150 percent) versus a narrow performance range (80-120 percent), and do the sides always have to be symmetrical (e.g., 50 percent above and below 100 percent or 20 percent above and below)? Part of the answer is mathematical, part is economic, part is psychological, and part is determined by your crystal ball.

First, the mathematical answers. As we discussed in chapter 14, lower-level employees typically have wider performance ranges than their team leaders and managers, who are managing toward an aggregate goal. This is due to something called the Law of Large Numbers (sometimes mistakenly called the Law of Averages). Basically, this means that for any individual, the probably of achieving the outcome of either 50 percent of goal or 150 percent of goal is about the same. But if we take ten people and add their results together, the probability now that the overall result of the team will be 50 percent of goal (in total) or 150 percent of goal (in total) diminishes; it is likely that some of the people will be above goal and some will be below goal, so the highs and the lows will average each other out, and the overall team result will land closer to the center of the curve or the expected value for the group as a whole. At each level of aggregation, you would get closer and closer to a center point. This means the odds of a manager or division or company's results landing far from the center are smaller, so you use a tighter performance range at each higher level of aggregation.

Secondly, consider the economic reasons. How much can you afford to pay at what level of performance? If you are replacing a straight commission paying from the first dollar, you can probably afford to have a very low threshold as that is what you have had so far. If you are adding incentive on top of salary for the first time, you may want to set a high threshold to ensure you are really gaining results for the additional dollars you are paying. Also, consider the costs on the upside. If you pay 200 percent of incentive at 120 percent of goal, will the 20 percent gained cover the additional 100 percent in incentive pay? (Remember to convert revenue to profit when testing plan economics, if you are using revenue as the goal.) You will likely be paying out a large percentage of the profit gain in compensation, but once you are above 100 percent of goal (if you've set your goals right), you should have covered all your fixed costs, and any additional profit will drop straight to the bottom line. You can afford to pay more, and in fact, it is worth it to pay more to encourage employees to get to that zone. It's better for you and it's better for them.

Thirdly, the psychological reasons. I've gone toe-to-toe with many a CFO over the need to pay incentive for anything below goal when they have a "bonus" or "profit-sharing" philosophy, where incentive payments are considered only as extra, or above and beyond, if goal is attained. While I get the economics of this philosophy[19], you've hampered the motivational value of your incentive plan if you take this approach. Good goal-setting should result in a bell curve of performance, with 50–60 percent of people at or above goal. This means 40–50 percent of people are below goal. Let's assume you have 100 people and each has a $1 million revenue goal. If forty of them increase their performance by 5 percent that's an additional $2 million in revenue ($50k × 40 people = $2 million or 2 percent of your overall goal). Check the math on the additional compensation cost to pay them for moving

---

[19] This philosophical debate also hinges a bit on where you set target total compensation. Did you design the plan so that market-competitive pay is achieved with salary alone, or are you depending on incentive pay to make up the difference? If the latter, this is not a "bonus" or "profit sharing" plan in the sense that a CFO might use those terms, but an incentive plan wherein the incentive acts as part of the employee's expected earnings. The difference between salary and incentive pay in this world is that the incentive varies based on performance and the salary is fixed. Some companies refer to these types of plans as VC plans (for "variable compensation") to clearly distinguish them from corporate profit sharing plans. VC plans are also more likely to be paid monthly or quarterly rather than once at the end of the year.

up 5 percent points, but I bet you that you will see it is worth it. If you make it so they have to get all the way to 100 percent of goal before payout, you will discourage nearly half of your population as they may feel it is "too far" to get to 100 percent; but, they might be able to get to 90 percent.

Finally, how good is your goal-setting? Are you 100 percent accurate in your future predictions of what is possible and what the economy will do? Probably not. To allow for some margin of error, you should have a range around goal that allows for unexpected windfalls or challenges. These can happen to any individual or to an entire company or industry. Providing a range gives your employees cushion on the downside, and you a bit of protection on the upside. Think of it this way: would you pay 200 percent of target incentive for 101 percent of goal? Probably not. So why would you pay 0 percent for 99 percent of goal?

From a practical standpoint, we commonly see percent ranges from 50-150 to 70-130 used for individual contributor roles and individual performance metrics. Likewise, we see 75-125 or 80-120 ranges for team metrics or team leader/manager goals. 90-110 ranges may be used for very high-level company goals. But, this begs one of our earlier questions. Do the ranges have to be symmetrical? No. Not at all. In high-growth situations (where the risk of backsliding is small and the risk of far exceeding goal is high) we may recommend a 90-150 range. Or, if you are putting someone into a turnaround situation with the high possibility of struggle and failure, a 50-110 range may make sense. It all depends on the circumstances. Typically, very large goals (such as for National Account Managers) have tighter ranges than very small goals. It is typically harder to achieve 120 percent growth on a $10 million goal than it is to achieve 120 percent growth on a $1 million goal.

But what happens above excellence? Again, sorry, it depends. If you are paying an individual for individual financial results, think long and hard before you cap the payout. Instead, consider a reduced slope or soft cap. In our 80-120 example above, the rate of change from 100 percent to 120 percent of goal was 5 percent of target incentive (5:1). In a soft-cap, we would cut the slope in half, so that any percent of goal above 120 percent is now worth 2.5 percent of target incentive (half of the 5 percent it was previously worth). This keeps the plan uncapped but puts protections in place for management in case of windfalls or flubbed goal setting. Note that you can also use a "deal cap" versus an overall cap. A deal cap limits the amount of credit that can be applied to goal from any single deal. This is often phrased as a percent of goal/quota (i.e., the maximum goal credit from any single deal will be 50 percent of the annual quota). This usually only comes into play for elephant-hunter-type roles that are doing large, multi-year transportation management or third party logistics (3PL) contacts, but it's worth remembering that it exists as an alternative to an overall cap.

However, if the element in question is non-financial or team based, then it probably should be capped. Otherwise, you run the risk of paying out an entire team for one person's good fortune, or you may overpay the value of the result gained if the measure is strategic with an imprecise link to financial results (such as new carriers or customers).

This concludes the discussion of the development of plan mechanics. We now have a full plan outline for our carrier sales role. In the remaining chapters, we will cover economic modeling (testing) of the new plans, communicating the plans, and the need for on-going plan administration and support.

SECTION V

Ensuring Your Beast Remains a Loyal and Faithful Companion

Chapter 19

Economic Modeling—No Surprises

Once you are done with your design and all of the mechanics, you still are not done. You need to test it to see how it works. I guarantee you will make changes. This is the "kicking the tires" phase of the design process, and it is one of the most difficult and most time consuming. You also need to have some pretty good Excel chops to be able to pull it off (or find someone who does). There are five levels of modeling you need to do, in the following order:

1. Calibration

2. Aggregate modeling

3. Incumbent scenario modeling

4. Incumbent historical modeling

5. Incumbent bridge planning

Calibration involves figuring out where to set your performance ranges, commission rates, and goals for the new compensation plan. Initially, as we discussed in the last chapter, this is based on some representative data to get you in the ballpark. The full economic modeling will take you deeper and prove out your results. Use Excel's percentile function to find your 10th, 25th, 50th, 75th, and 90th percentile performances on the various measures you are using. With this exercise, you are defining what "good" looks like and the economic value you gain from "good" (and "great"). This helps you work through the details of the payout tables for each individual element in your plan. When you are putting in a new measure (such as number of new customers) you may not have good historical data to work with. In this case, you should call on the best managerial minds in your organization and ask them what "good" looks like. Now is not a time to find people who will tell you what you want to hear: "Yeah, boss, a good sales rep should bring in 100 new customers a month and a good carrier sales rep should move fifty loads a day." *Not!* You need reality, and you need to know if you are out-of-whack in your expectations. If you put an incentive plan in place that has unrealistic expectations you will, at best, have wasted all the time and effort (and money) on the design process and, at worst, demoralized your entire staff and caused them all to quit. Be careful on this and don't get greedy. A journey of a thousand miles begins with a single step.

The second phase of economic modeling is aggregate modeling. This takes the total amount you will pay to your staff under the plan (salary + all incentives) and divides it by the total financial results you will get from your staff under the plan. The answer for what is "right" here varies tremendously, and when I hear such precise answers as 33.33 percent, I just laugh. Who is included in the numbers (just production staff or all admin support)? What type of freight? What's the sales model? There are many right answers to the overall cost of compensation as a percent of profit. I've worked with healthy companies where this ratio is 18 percent (excluding *all* admin support as they were covered by the parent, an asset-based company, and they had tons of EDI freight) and healthy companies where this ratio is north of 50 percent (including all admin support resources and dealing with high-value, high-touch freight).

It really depends, and you are being too simplistic if you think there is one number that is "right" for all brokers. What you do want to see is a decrease in the ratio at higher levels of performance and over time. As your staff increases the production per head, your cost of compensation should drop (because you are covering any fixed costs you have in the form of salary). Over time you should be increasing both the production expectation and the payout, but the former should be going up at a faster rate than the latter. Astute readers at this point will recognize a problem with a straight commission plan.

What I just described as the desired economic outcome can *never* happen if you pay using a flat commission plan with no salary. It's mathematically impossible unless you reduce the commission rate over time. If you are one of the few brokers left paying 30 percent commission with no salary, your employees will get rich while you fail to receive the reward for your investment in the company. You will have invested in high-end marketing, a good office building, top-of-the-line equipment, programmers to develop a kick-butt TMS system, support resources to process invoices and enter and track loads, but who really benefits? The rep making 30 percent on everything he produces.

Just think for a minute. Is it harder or easier for a rep to produce under the situation I described? Certainly easier. The company invested a ton of money to make it easier on them. The gain should be shared. Yes, the company is making its 70 percent, but relatively speaking, they are investing more and more of that money and getting less and less back for it.

So, to get your aggregate economic modeling right (after you've wisely moved away from a straight commission model), you need to gather the business KPIs from chapter 3 and put them all in one place (we use one tab in our Excel model called "Company Goals" to collect this info and break it down as needed). As a quick refresher, these KPIs included:

- Company goals such as revenue, profit, profit percent, revenue per load, profit per load, total loads, number of new customers, and any other metrics being measured in the incentive plan

- All of the above goals broken down to division, branch or reasonable business unit

- Actual historical results for the last two years for all of the above numbers

Look at the prior two year's performance and next year's goals. Consider the gap between last year's performance and next year's performance. How big is the gap? Can your existing staff close it or do you need to hire more people? It may help to gather your "Productivity Expectations" for each role and multiply them by the number of existing and planned hires for each role. You want to multiply and then sum (use Excel's SUMPRODUCT function to make this easy) and see if it all adds up. What is the gap to the company goals? What is the expected average load count per day per role? Is this reasonable based on what they have historically accomplished? Are you planning for new hires to help close the gap or are you going to install a better TMS system to help increase efficiency? If you are planning to hire new people, be sure to consider that you will have to cover 100 percent of their costs before you are getting 100 percent performance from them. Brokers are very familiar with a ramp up schedule—use that schedule when estimating your performance from new hires, *but* cut it in half—as most ramp-up schedules I've seen are still too aggressive.

One caution when doing the modeling: be sure to consider both sides if you have a functionally split organization model. This means you cannot add the sum of the shipper sales productivity to the sum of the carrier sales productivity and get your company number. You will be overstating by as much as 2×. It may be less than 2× so you may not be able to simply take the sum and divided by 2, if sometimes the shipper resources cover their own loads, or if sometimes loads come in through EDI that go straight to a carrier resource, or if there are house accounts that are not assigned to a sales resource. It requires some thought and understanding of how loads flow through your system to be sure you are getting the numbers right.

Once you are comfortable with the aggregate results—simply answering "can you do it with the planned resources for an estimated cost that is reasonable"—then you need to move to the incumbent scenario modeling. This takes each plan design and calculates payout for each of your people at the individual level, including proposed new hires, using the exact measures and mechanics of the new plan under at least six different performance levels. We typically use two levels below target, target (which is your anchor point), and three levels above target. You should run these results and get two sets of numbers for each of the six scenarios: (1) total compensation: (salary, which won't change) + incentive (which will increase for higher levels of performance) and (2) company profit generated.

As you compare the results for the six scenarios (and to your historical baseline) you should see that your total cost of compensation as percent of-profit is reducing at higher levels of performance. If it doesn't, you need to look at the rate of acceleration that you have in your mechanics at high ends of performance and probably back them down a bit. Also, consider the relative payout at target to what you have historically paid. It may be higher or lower but it should be what you want. If it is lower, is it too low? Will your staff feel this is too much of a takeaway? If it is higher, is this because you are consciously investing in compensation to get yourself closer to market? Both answers can be right under different circumstances, but both need to be understood completely and planned for in terms of change management.

If the economics are not coming up right, and they rarely do the first time around, you may need to dig into the individual roles and metrics to find the source of any problem. Hopefully, the issue is not systemic but limited to one or two roles that you can fine tune now that you see the problem. Doing it this way will also give you a view into how your employees will perceive the new plan. At target, who is making more or less than their old plan? Why? Is the change justified? If someone is making less, how far above target do they have to go to be whole? Does this correspond to their current level of performance? You can't compare an excellent prior year performance to modeled target performance and expect the person to make the same amount—but you can, and should, compare excellence to excellence and see if things balance out then.

The next level of modeling is the most fun (yes, I'm a bit warped), but it really is fun and it's absolutely the most important. This is called individual historic modeling. For this, you need to take the actual performance from the prior year for each person and run it through the new plan designs. Now you will see who really would make more and who would make less, because it's no longer hypothetical. Don't worry if you can't model all of it. We always have to make some guesses or assumptions for some of the elements, because historical data simply doesn't exist. That's OK. Just keep it in mind when drawing conclusions about the plans—there is some margin of error in the analysis. Be sure to consider performance period impacts; are you shifting from discrete quarterly to quarterly with an annual true-up? This change will change the payouts even if everything else is the same, because more will be back end loaded with a true-up and you may have some cash flow concerns from your staff. Consider changes in salary as well—if you are increasing someone's salary, that will offset a loss in incentives. Are you shifting from exempt to non-exempt and need to consider the impact of overtime pay on the total package? Once you have the historic modeling done, you need to "gut-check" it with your management team. They know your people and their results and abilities, probably better than you do. Have them sense-check the data (are your performance inputs right? They often aren't. Is the historical pay data right? It often isn't). You need to be sure you are comparing apples to apples as much as possible, and then consider, are the right people "winning" and right people "losing" under this plan? Your managers know the answers. If it's coming up wrong, you may have disproportionate emphasis in some areas of the plan (go back and change your weights) or you may be increasing goals too much and instead need to hire more people. There are always changes to the plan design at this point. Always.

The last level of modeling is individual bridge-plan modeling, and it is not always needed. If you are adding incentives without reducing salaries, you can skip this paragraph, as few will be upset by the change.[20] If you are changing from more frequent payouts to less frequent payouts and have any significant amount of pay at risk, you absolutely need to consider bridge plans. If you are changing from commission plans to goal-based plans (even if this involves a salary increase) you will need to take extra time with your bridge planning and communication. For the record, changing a straight-commission plan to nearly any other type of plan is the most difficult change to make and one of the reasons why we dislike them so much. They create the wrong economic outcomes (payouts are too extreme for the employees and out of balance with the company) and they are nearly impossible to change—so you find yourself stuck with a very bad plan design. If you at least have a goal-based or tiered commission, you have a fighting chance of being able to make a change that will keep the economics in balance.

The most common cause for needing a bridge plan is a change in payout timing. You used to pay monthly and now you are going to pay quarterly. Or you used to pay bi-weekly and now want to pay monthly. All of these situations limit how quickly you can change. People have bills to pay and are used to getting their incentive checks on a particular frequency. You may also need a bridge plan if you are moving people into a role that will require some ramp-up before incentive payments start to hit (such as under a bank or bounty plan for inside sales). Typically, the best approach here is to create a graduated guarantee scale using the employee's prior 12-month average pay. Guarantee they will make at least as much as they made in the prior year per period, and pay that amount for the first three performance periods under the new plan. Calculate the incentive under the new plan, and if it is more, pay the extra. If it is less, pay the higher historical amount. For the next three periods, reduce the guarantee by 25 percent or 50 percent. Then reduce again. This way, after six to nine periods, the person has transitioned to the new plan and should have been able to get personal finances aligned so that car payments, mortgages, etc. can be made out of the savings from the less-frequent incentive payments.

This is not dissimilar to what you may do with new hires; there is, however, one important note I'd like to make here. You should not raise their salary and then reduce it (either for a new hire or for a bridge plan). Instead, guarantee a minimum incentive payout and then reduce that. Mathematically, it's the same, but psychologically it's very different. Salary takes on meaning for a person; it is more than just dollars. When you reduce salary, you are telling them they are valued less. Plus, when you guarantee the incentive and then reduce it, you are lining up what is being reduced (the guaranteed incentive) with what is being increased (the incentive they should be earning on their own). We find it much better to keep the salary in its own sandbox and not to intermingle those dollars with incentive dollars in any way (recall the discussion about this from chapter 4).

---

[20] Interestingly, we have seen people upset by an added incentive plan as they were resistant to being measured and rated. Clients have described this effect as similar to turning the lights on in an old kitchen and seeing the roaches run to the corners.

This gets you about 75 percent of the way done with your new compensation plan. Only 75 percent? What?! Sorry, but it's true. There are three big steps left to cover that will be at least as much work as what you've already gone through: goal-setting, communicating the plan, and administering the plan. We will cover goal-setting next. (Note: if you are not using individualized (relative) goals, you can skip this chapter or save it for a future date).

Chapter 20

Goal Setting—The Art and the Science

This chapter will not be relevant for everyone. If you are using standard performance expectations (e.g., $10,000 per month in GP$ per carrier sales rep), a straight commission plan, or even a commission plan with fixed-dollar tiers, you can skip this chapter. If you are using customized goals which vary by individual, then you will need to read this. Throughout this series we have been using Carrier Sales as our sample role. It is unlikely that you would want to set individualized goals for your carrier sales force. It's possible, if you have many different types of freight, but even so, you are still likely to find yourself gravitating to standard performance expectations by freight type rather than by individual.

Where individual goal setting comes into play is in the traditional outside sales world with geographic territory assignments that are inherently unequal in opportunity. Using fixed productivity expectations in this world causes all kinds of problems—such as over or underpaying and demoralizing the sales force. Note that a straight-commission plan carries with it a presumed fixed productivity expectation; the only difference is you are letting your sales reps decide their own productivity expectation based on how much money they want to make. You have no way of ensuring that when the reps hit their goals, the company will reach its goals, as you don't know what their goals actually are. Therefore, when you are dealing with a sales force with unequal opportunities and you want to be sure you are paying the market rate for the jobs (based on effort and ability) and that the team performance will equal an overall company objective, using individualized goals is the right way to go.

There are some simple ways to set goals, and some more complex ways. And you guessed it; the more complex ways yield a better outcome. The reps are bought into the goal-setting process, the goals are perceived as more fair, and the goals are better aligned with company performance. But we'll go through the simple methods first, as they all build to the more complex (and preferred) method.

Option #1: Top Down, Even Allocation

This one is really easy and is not really individualized goal setting. Say you have a company goal of $10 million and you have ten reps. Under this method, each rep carries a goal of $1 million. Wow—did I blow your mind with the complexity there? You can vary this approach by breaking the higher level goals down by region, division, freight type etc. but the fundamental math is still the same. At some point you take a big number and divide it by the number of reps and that determines the goal. This method may work if the reps all truly have the ability to each generate $1 million (often the case for inside sales due to a level playing field), but if you have outside sales and one is in North Dakota and another in New York, I guarantee they don't have a level playing field.

Option #2: Even Growth Percent Expectation over Historical Baseline

In this case the company needs to grow 10 percent. So every rep's prior year performance is increased by 10 percent—boom—you have an individualized goal. Well, sort of. What about the rep who achieved a record year last year? Are you really going to expect her to grow 10 percent on top of that? What about a rep who lost 50 percent of his business? Are you going to expect him to just regain 10 percent of the 50 percent loss (and reward that?). Also, 10 percent of a large, mature territory may be nearly impossible, whereas it may be very easy for a small relatively unpenetrated territory. You can see this method will create some problems.

Option #3: Even Allocation of Growth Dollars to Historical Baseline

To balance out the large territory/small territory issue in Option #2, some companies use a blend of #1 and #2. They decide the company wants to grow by $1 million (10 percent of $10 million), and they have 10 reps, so each rep should have $100,000 ($1 million/10) added to his or her prior-year performance. While this does normalize the growth expectation a bit ($100,000 for the rep with the $2 million territory is better than the $200,000 you'd get with the 10 percent approach), you have now created the opposite problem for small territories. If you had a rep who only did $100,000 last year (maybe the one in North Dakota), you are now saying he or she has to double production to hit goal. OK—so we are not quite there yet.

Option #4: Take Option #2 or #3 Using The Prior Two-Year Average as Baseline

This helps with something we call *porpoiseing* (like a dolphin)—a good year results in too high a goal the following year, which creates a bad year, which then results in an easier goal the next year, etc. When you use a two-year average as the baseline, you balance out good and bad years and won't punish a rep who had a great second year; neither will you reward a rep with an easy goal following a year in which the rep's performance tanked.

Option #5: Bottom-up Goal Setting

Under this method, you ask your sales force to set their own goals based on account knowledge, market knowledge, etc. The risk here is obvious—sandbagging. Suddenly, the outlook on the world will get very dark. They are going to have to walk uphill both ways to call on their clients, through snow and sleet and hail, and all their clients are suddenly on the verge of bankruptcy. In all likelihood, when you add the goals together from this method, they will not equal the overall company goal (they may not even be *close*).

It should be obvious by now that none of the options outlined above is ideal. So what's the best answer? Combine them and create a weighted average, and (this is the important part) get your sales staff involved in the process. Have them pick the options to use and get their inputs on how the weights should be assigned for the weighted average. This may sound complex, but it's actually not. It takes a bit more time, but the payoff in terms of buy-in to the goal-setting process is well worth it. Let me walk through an example:

Let's say the team decides to use #2, #3, #4 with growth percent, and #5. And they will weight them as follows:

Option 2: 10 percent growth percent over prior year (weight: 20 percent)

Option 3: $100,000 even $ growth allocation over prior year (weight: 20 percent)

Option 4: 15 percent growth percent over prior two-year average (weight: 30 percent)

Option 5: Sales rep goal allocation (weight: 30 percent)

Next, we figure out what the goal should be. Let's say a rep did $800,000 two years ago and $1,200,000 last year. The rep's goals would come out as follows:

Option 2: $1,200,000 × 110 percent = $1,320,000 × 20 percent weight = $264,000

Option 3: $1,200,000 + $100,000 = $1,300,000 × 20 percent weight = $260,000

Option 4: ($800,000 + $1,200,000)/2 = $1,000,000 × 115 percent = $1,150,000 × 30 percent = $345,000

Option 5: The sales rep says the world is a terrible place and he or she will only be able to do $1 million next year: $1,000,000 × 30 percent = $300,000

The sum of these goals is $1,169,000. The rep may be a little disgruntled because the goal is higher than he or she wanted, but it's far less than Option 2 or 3 alone would have yielded, and provides the chance to see continued reward from a strong recent year (provided the world truly isn't as dark as he or she put forth).

You will have to check that all the goals determined this way add to the overall company number that is required. They probably won't (due to sandbagging in Option 5). If this is the case, you will need to go back to the reps to ask for them to each take on some of the gap that is left (or if the gap is small, you might now reasonably divide it among the reps in an even fashion). Some companies get creative at this point and they look at how much t' sandbagged. Those who shot low in their estimation take on a larger portion of the those who ponied up more at the start. This also teaches reps not to sandbag—af' year, they will realize it backfires on them at the end of the process.

If you have a large, hierarchical sales force with VPs, Regional Managers, District Managers, etc., then you need to cascade the process through each level, first getting the VPs to accept their goals, then the RMs, who then get DSMs to accept their goals, who finally get reps to accept their goals. This way there is alignment all the way up and down the chain and no one had a goal forced on them. Plus, every person saw all of the inputs and weights and understands why the goals came out the way they did.

As I said at the start, yes—this is more complex and more time consuming than using one method in isolation, but it provides a far better outcome.

In the next chapters, we will address the best methods for communicating the new compensation plans to employees, and how to administer and manage them throughout the year (both parts *are just as important* as the design process).

Chapter 21

Change Management Lessons from the Compensation Front-Lines

In the last two decades, I have seen nearly everything when it comes to the highs and lows of implementing new initiatives. There are few topics more personal than compensation, and therefore, all compensation consultants learn how to manage the psychological impact of these changes early in their careers. This experience has led me to develop a framework that can be used for any change initiative to help management chart a safer course through the treacherous waters of change-management.

When rolling out a change initiative, it's helpful to understand the psychology of the members of the affected group. The Vocality/Predisposition Matrix (VPM) (below) can help managers identify (before and after the change) those parties who may need some extra attention to help get them over the hump of accepting the new program.

Table 21.1: *Vocality/Predisposition Matrix*

		Predisposition Toward Change initiative	
		Positive	**Negative**
Approach to Expressing Opinions in Group Settings (Vocality)	**Vocal**	• Genuinely enthusiastic supporters of management initiatives • Highly loyal to the company • Top performers who are well respected by others	• Unlikely to like any change put in front of them • Heavy negotiators who work every angle to their own benefit (not infrequently, top sales reps are in this group) • May have the respect of others in the organization, particularly if they are top performers • Less likely to sway others if they are perceived as perpetual doomsayers on all issues
	NonVocal	• Will follow the crowd and not take a strong stand one way or the other • Has a high degree of trust in management • May ask a few questions or seek clarification, but the questions will be driven by a genuine desire to understand rather than to poke holes	• Will not speak up during management-led discussion of change, but will express negative feelings behind the scenes in one-on-one conversations • Classic passive/aggressive behaviors may be common (if asked, will say they like the idea, but later change opinion or qualify statement) • Can be the most damaging to the organization especially if any of the ones in this bucket are top performers

The value in this insight is the ability it gives management to get in front of the challenges and opportunities different types of employees offer. There are three critical times when management must use this tool.

- When establishing the business case for change

- When preparing for the rollout of the change

- When enacting the change itself, following rollout (especially in the critical first days)

Establishing the Business Case for Change

When preparing for a large change, whatever the topic, management should engage employees in defining the challenge and suggesting solutions. This can be done through surveys, interviews, and/or focus groups; all methods are beneficial as they allow employees a chance to vent and to express their concerns about the potential upheaval the change may cause. We always recommend including one Vocal-Positive and one Vocal-Negative employee as part of the interview or focus group process for developing new ideas. It is particularly important to include top performers in this group, as they will be likely to sway Nonvocal-Neutrals. They *also* represent the greatest risk to the organization if the change is managed badly and becomes the proximate cause of their departure from the organization. It is important that any interviews, focus groups, or surveys are conducted by a trusted third party who does not have hiring, firing, salary review, or any other authority over those being interviewed, and who will keep all information confidential. There must be enough interviews that outcomes can be reported without identifying the source of any particular comment. Findings should be reported in aggregate and should focus on things that directly impact the proposed course of action for the change rather than rooting out naysayers.

Preparing for the Rollout

Organizations go through all types of changes, from small-group impact to organization-wide changes. Some changes are fairly impersonal (changing a corporate logo) and others are deeply personal (compensation and benefits). The types of changes that will most benefit from the use of the VPM will be initiatives that affect a contained group (such as your sales force) on a topic that naturally arouses passion (such as compensation) and where the risk to your organization is high if the change does not go well (which is why sales compensation is one of the front-line training grounds for anyone wanting to jump into the deep end of change management).

As management is organizing the rollout, give consideration to ensuring the non-vocals will have time to be heard. For example, new sales compensation plans can be rolled out with a high degree of pomp and circumstance at the national sales meeting in a large conference center auditorium, or they can be rolled out in smaller groups over the course of several days. In either case, you need to plan some one-on-one time with each employee so he or she can voice his or her concerns or issues outside of the group setting.

Generally, groups with like interests should be kept together so there is limited confusion or discussion of topics that are not relevant to a part of the audience. If management is slotting people into groups based on function or level, consider splitting up the Vocals so you have at least one Positive and no more than one Negative in each group meeting. You also want a balance of the Nonvocals, and you want to be sure to group Nonvocal-Negatives with as many positive influences as possible. One of the fastest ways to suck the life out of your presenter and his or her ability to generate enthusiasm for your new compensation plan is for him or her to look out upon a sea of employees with their arms crossed across their chests and read nothing but expressions of doubt, resentment, or downright hostility on their faces.

Another common mistake companies make is to schedule the rollout and then allow key players not to be present. Some circumstances are genuinely unavoidable (illness or emergency), but any significant change should be scheduled well enough in advance so the employees can work their vacation or discretionary time away from the office around the critical day or days. To the extent possible, the rollout should be done live with as many affected participants as possible. In this world of increasing technology dependence, we forget the value of delivering news face-to-face. You cannot read body language over a webinar, and even if you have cameras set up, it's still not as good as the real thing. If the change is important to the organization, it's important to make the effort to get people together for it. For example, a rollout in Asia that we were involved in, while only affecting thirty or so sales reps, was still taken seriously enough by management that all participants, presenters, and managers were flown from Korea and China to Thailand to participate in the rollouts.

For a particularly challenging change initiative, it may be a good idea to call in the reserves. Conduct a challenge team meeting of key team leaders, managers, and/or top performers. Give them a chance to help you craft the communications materials (at this stage, make it clear they are not able to change the direction or affect the content of the compensation plans materially; presumably those decisions have already been made). Enlisting their support before the change is communicated to the broader audience can prove invaluable when it comes time for the rollout. This group will be primed with answers and will have had a chance to raise, and resolve, their key concerns and misunderstandings. If you plan for them to have a part in the official rollout, this will visibly show their support, but even better is if their support naturally emerges during the rollout in a more spontaneous (and less scripted) fashion.

After the Rollout

During and after the rollout, keep an eye out for who has changed camps. There will be some surprises. The topic for this change initiative may be something that causes a passionate response from one of your otherwise Nonvocals. Or a Vocal may be having an off day and does not step up to the role you expected him or her to play. Be absolutely certain you have done your homework about how the change will affect each individual. One of the worst experiences is to roll out a new program that you think will be well received, only to find you've missed some critical piece of information or had an incorrect piece of information. In the data-intensive and minute-detail-oriented world of sales compensation, this happens with almost every rollout. Someone's salary was misstated in a data file, their productivity numbers were significantly higher or lower than what was used to model the new payouts due to a glitch or restatement in the accounting system, they have a signed letter from the VP of Sales promising them a certain minimum incentive payout for a period that extends into the new plan year, etc. Obviously, once raised, these issues must be acknowledged honestly and addressed and corrected immediately.

You will need to plan for follow-up discussions with any high-performing Nonvocal-Negatives immediately following the group meeting. They will be formulating in their heads the reasons why the new initiative won't work, and you will want to address these concerns directly and work through any misconceptions (which there will be) and legitimate concerns *before* they have a chance to express these feelings in semi-hushed conversations with their co-workers or via email. If the change issue is pay, be sure you have your ducks in a row. Know what they have been paid in the past several years, how this new change is likely to affect them, and what they need to do to remain whole. Let them know you have already considered their concerns and put yourself in their shoes. If the change involves a shift in the mix of total rewards, be sure to quantify as many of the elements as you can so they are not left to fill in the blanks about what the change really means to them. For example, if you are shifting to a more variable pay mix, which means reducing base salaries, be sure you have bridge plans ready and can explain how your employees are expected to meet their monthly expenses until the first incentive check comes. If you are instituting a different or more lucrative car allowance program, be sure you are up on the tax implications; what sounds great to you might not come across that way to your sales force, especially if they regularly put more than 100,000 miles on their car each year. Data are difficult to argue with. Know the facts *before* having the meetings, and be genuinely compassionate about your employee's concerns.

In the end, if handled well, the bulk of your organization will get through the change. You may have some heated debates with your Vocal-Negatives. And if they are in sales, negotiation is just part of their job description (you likely would not want them in the sales force if they *didn't* try to negotiate the best deal possible). Have the passion, the smarts, and the leadership backing to stand toe-to-toe with them if needed. For others, the change initiative may be more than they can handle and may finally bring to a head the problems with their attitude. In the end, if your Vocal-Negatives can't support the new system, then it may be time to let them go; the damage these types can do to the motivation and morale of a company can be profound. Don't be timid about making staffing changes based on the VPM. It's rare that a person with an inherently negative attitude is ever a long-term asset to a company. An organizational change can be a great way to bring these issues to light and give you the ammunition you need to clean house.

Chapter 22

Document Your Plans to Prevent Costly Confusion

The joke goes that the majority of incentive plans are drawn up by the company president and sales director hastily over cocktails and written on a napkin. While a bit more thought is put into most incentive compensation plans than this, there is a kernel of truth beneath the folklore, and the place this is most often evident is in the plan document—the piece of paper given to employees to explain how they are going to be paid.

The risks of poorly-documented incentive compensation plans range from your employees not understanding the plan (and therefore not being motivated by it), to legal battles with former employees who claim they are owed back-incentive pay due to vague, inaccurate, or misleading wording in the plan document.

At a minimum, a well-written plan document must have the following components:

- **Plan Overview:** This part describes plan objectives, who is eligible, the timeframe during which the plan will be effective, what the target incentive amount is at 100 percent performance, and a high-level view of the characteristics of the various elements of the plan: weight, target incentive, pay frequency, and performance period.

- **Element Details:** This section thoroughly explains each plan element, and details the method used to calculate results (e.g., "Gross profit is calculated by subtracting the cost of purchased transportation services from the customer payment, excluding adjustments for discounts and fuel surcharges"). Wording must be precise to prevent misunderstanding. Include commission rates, commission tables, bonus payout tables, and any other information that will enable employees to quickly and easily calculate their own incentive payments. Be sure to also document any qualifiers that must be met before pay will be earned (e.g., "An individual's monthly average gross profit percent must be 10 percent to earn incentives under this measure"). If modifiers are part of the plan, include them in the plan document at this point as well (e.g., "If your on-time percentage falls below 95 percent, your incentive for the performance period will be reduced by 50 percent"). Include information about any quotas that will be used to determine pay, and provide a calculation example so the employees can follow it step-by-step[21].

---

[21] Do not include goals in the plan doc—just use generic examples as you do not want the administrative burden of individualized plan docs that need to be updated with each goal change.

- **Plan Policies and Practices:** This is the very important legal disclaimer section that is often completely omitted. Things to include in this section are policies about payment when an employee transfers, is on leave or is terminated. Preparing this plan document section will force you to think about how you would handle incentive payouts in each of these cases *before* they happen, which could save you a lot of money *after* they happen. Also, be clear about when incentives are earned. Are they *earned* when a load ships, is delivered, is invoiced, or when it is paid? If an employee terminates and a load that shipped while the employee was active is paid after termination, will that employee still be entitled to be paid for that load? Check with your labor attorney on this, as local laws governing commissions vary.

Also include disclaimers that the incentive plan is not a guarantee of employment, that management has the right to modify the plan at any time and for any reason, with or without notice, and that management may adjust sales credit and/or payout at its sole discretion to preserve fairness to the company and the employee.

Credit-splitting and adjustments must be clearly outlined either here or under the pertinent Element Details section. If you have not documented your policies in these two areas, now is an excellent time. Consider the situation if two parties work the same load, handle the same customer, cover for each other when one is on vacation or out to lunch, etc. Also, what happens if there is a major adjustment after you've already paid the incentive? What about bad-debt write-offs? Is there a cut-off point beyond which a load will no longer be eligible for incentives (e.g., must be paid within sixty, ninety, 120 days)? The list goes on.

If there is any possibility of collusion or kickbacks, either between your staff and customers or carriers, or among your staff, be sure to include a clause that such behavior will result in immediate termination. Include a confidentiality clause and a funding clause that allows management the right to suspend payment on the plan if overall business conditions are unfavorable (although we recommend using this clause as a last resort only; if it is invoked for reasons other than impending insolvency, then you have a disincentive plan rather than an incentive plan).

Finally, review the whole Plan Policies and Practices section to be sure your intentions are accurately and unambiguously stated; if you do not state your intentions clearly, your ex-employee will likely make an interpretation in his or her favor, and this could land you in court.

Once your plan document accurately reflects your intentions to the best of your ability, have it reviewed by legal counsel. It will be seen in many jurisdictions as a contract and is worthy of a legal review. While your lawyer's contribution is important, you may want to consider reminding him or her that this is supposed to be a motivating and exciting document, understandable by the eligible employee.

The thought required to develop each of these sections will result in better plan designs, prevent costly challenges, and help ensure your employees understand how they will be paid under the plan. A well-written plan document will help ensure your well-designed plan focuses effort on the results your business needs.

Chapter 23

Beyond Cash Compensation: Motivation and Morale on a Tight Budget

One approach some transportation and logistics companies take when dealing with a recession is to eliminate incentive compensation and revert to a 100-percent-salary approach, which gives them the ability to manage to a fixed cost of compensation and deal with productivity and staffing from a purely 1:1 perspective—if a person isn't generating enough to justify his salary, he won't stay around very long.

This is not a position that can be (or should be) maintained for long in this industry. Carrier sales, inside sales reps, customer service reps, account managers, and outside sales reps have too much bottom-line impact on the business (prominence) to be on a 100-percent salary plan. Incentive compensation should be used as a strategic lever to drive the results the business needs and to reward those who are performing at the top of their game, which will in turn, make the company an attractive place to work for other top performers.

Under improved market conditions, many companies revamp their compensation approach, adding variable pay back into the mix, but they are often leery about the negatives they've seen from too much emphasis on individual incentives and not enough emphasis on teamwork, accuracy, follow-up, and good old customer service.

Similarly, smart managers recognize that their staff may have been bounced from one extreme to another and that a full swing back to a highly variable program would be too much for them to take. Furthermore, a 100-percent-variable plan might preclude some good hires; many people are leery of accepting any position without a salary, given what appears to be the new norm in terms of high market volatility.

There are also budget issues to consider. It may not be practical or possible to just add incentive compensation on top of current salary levels—but then management has a "new," "exciting," and supposedly "motivational" incentive program that starts with the information that salaries are being cut to make room for the incentives. Such a conversion is not impossible, and we have helped clients through this, but it *is very* hard to build excitement from this starting point.

So, what are some alternatives? How can you get the motivation and morale you need to drive performance and reduce complacency without breaking your budget or forcing deep salary cuts? The answer may lie in the balanced use of contests (SPIFFs) and recognition programs, alongside a more modest team- and goal-oriented incentive pay program. (By the way, legend has it that SPIFF stands for **S**pecial **P**erformance **I**ncentive **F**or the **F**ield, but I don't think anyone really knows for sure what it stands for.) It's a recommended best practice for any company (no matter where they are in moving toward or away from a more variable compensation program) to use contests and recognition programs to supplement rewards and drive behavior; for companies that are trying to reintroduce incentives, this can be a safe and highly cost-effective way to begin.

Many sales organizations use a President's Club (or something similar) to recognize those employees who are consistently performing at a high level. There is usually some immediate reward, such as an all-expenses-paid trip for the employee and his or her spouse, but there can also be an ongoing reward that encourages continued performance at this level. One of my clients outside of this industry has a tiered, retroactive commission program: the rate starts out at a lower level and moves up with production throughout the year. As a reward for making President's Club in a given year, all members start their next year's incentive program on the second tier, which creates a powerful motivator to stay in the club during subsequent years as it reduces the pain in January when the rate resets at the lowest rate. One large broker makes the use of their game room during work hours as one of their President's Club membership privileges (and this room has a glass wall that looks into the brokerage floor, which makes it motivational for those who would also like to be able to use the facilities). A standard practice at many other companies is to designate a preferred parking spot for the top producer in a given period.

These programs, however, are not without their challenges and risks. Some companies can become SPIFF-happy and end up paying out more money in SPIFFs than they do in the regular incentive program. This can quickly make your CFO very unhappy, as your cost of compensation will likely skyrocket beyond justified levels. One client came to us because their incentive plan was so terribly broken, no more than 30 percent of the employees on the plan were earning any incentive under what was a highly-variable program (as we have discussed prior in this book, you want 90 percent of your employees to get *something*, and 50–60 percent to earn target payouts or better). To solve the problem, the Sales Director had instituted monthly and quarterly SPIFFs that were filling in gaps and ensuring employees were able to pay their bills and continue working for the company. Obviously this was not a good use of SPIFFs and the sales force was waiting to make sales until they found out what the next monthly or quarterly SPIFF was going to be. In this case, the right answer was to fix the broken compensation plan by ensuring productivity expectations were realistic given market conditions.

Another problem can arise when the recognition program rewards results that are counter to the incentive program. A very large furniture manufacturer had a President's Club that depended on revenue produced. Their incentive program was profit-based. I don't need to explain to anyone in the logistics world why this was a problem. Their existing incentive program was so weak, and their President's Club so culturally strong that no one paid much attention to profit at all. This is a good cautionary tale about the potential power of recognition programs; they work, but they can sometimes work counter to the good of the organization if not managed properly.

The bottom line is to take a thoughtful and holistic approach to all parts of your compensation program: salary and incentive compensation (including the proper ratio between them), contests (SPIFFs), and recognition programs. You don't need to overdo the contests and recognition programs to get results, but their consistent and balanced use can increase staff motivation and enable you to focus on the most immediate business needs while you make more gradual adjustments to your salary and incentive compensation programs.

Chapter 24

Getting Results that Last

Now that we have designed the plan, tested it with economic modeling, and communicated it to the staff, we can sit back and rake in the cash, right?

Wrong.

Your new compensation plan requires a tremendous amount of care and feeding if you are to gain anything from all the time and money you've invested so far. Should you think at this point you are done, and it is someone else's problem, you are sorely mistaken, my friend. No more than you can spend hours researching the best gym in town, sign up for the highest level of membership, buy the most expensive workout clothes, and hire the most reputable personal trainer, and expect to get into better shape without actually going to the gym and working out.

First, you need to deal with the ongoing change management your people need. Not everyone will respond the same way. Some will be enthusiastic and some will be wary. Nearly everyone will misunderstand something about the plan and need clarification and additional explanation after the first few paychecks. We always warn clients that people don't really understand a new plan until they have received two checks from it. The first check has about a 50/50 shot of reaffirming any mistaken ideas they have about the plan, but when they get the second check, you will find out how close or far off they are in their interpretation of the plan and how the math works. We have worked for months with a design team only to have them send us their calculations at the end of the first pay period showing they interpreted the math in a very different way than we intended. It may not be *wrong*, and sometimes we have developed creative new incentive approaches from this, but it certainly can be *different*. And these were people who sat in the room with us as we discussed in extended detail how each part of the plan worked.

It never ceases to amaze me the different levels of interpretation you can get when talking about incentive compensation, even after you have walked through an example step-by-step. Just be prepared for many different interpretations from your staff, even the ones who told you from the outset they got it (maybe *especially* from them).

Second, you need to make sure you are prepared to run calculations and get checks to the staff as soon as possible after the pay period has closed. The worst thing you can do is not pay people after the start of a new plan. We worked with a client one time who spent more than five months developing the new plan, ran it for one month, and then refused to pay the staff their earned incentives because he didn't see a change in their attitudes in the first month. Hmm. I think maybe the problem with their attitudes was not caused by the incentive plan. Needless to say, he didn't feel he'd gotten the benefit he expected from the plan. This is a bit like expecting to go to the gym one time and lose 100 lbs.; it's not going to happen. The process takes time, and it takes time for people to adapt to and internalize the change. If you are too quick to pull the plug or if you make major changes in the first few months of the plan, you will never see the results you can get otherwise.

Third, you need to be prepared to make adjustments. There will be unexpected consequences, and you should be prepared to make small tweaks as needed. No incentive plan is 100 percent perfect, and every good plan needs adjusting—either to unforeseen circumstances or to longer-term changes in the economic conditions of the world or your business. If you have participated in the process up to this point, then you will understand how to manipulate the new tool you have. Change a weight here, a goal there, dial this up and that down. You will fine-tune the plan to make it work for you and your staff. Tweaking does not mean the plan was broken—it means you learned what you needed to learn to keep the plan working for you rather than the other way around.

Fourth, you need to get results in front of your people. Emphasize the results and celebrate successes as they happen. We've seen large-screen TVs put up around the office showing daily rankings and results, and we've seen managers hand out sheets of paper at the end of the week to show employees how they are tracking on their plan. Either low-tech or high-tech works; you just need to be sure your staff knows how they are doing while they can still change the outcome. If they only find out after the pay period is over, they will be less motivated because they can't change the outcome now. Sure, they can do better next time, but, in terms of driving motivation, feedback during the pay cycle is far superior in terms of driving motivation to feedback given only after the fact.

There are software programs available to provide dashboards and automated calculations, but most of them cannot handle the complexity of transportation sales. Most were built for large-scale sales organizations in which one person is credited for a sale (not two or three). If you are interested, you can research "Enterprise Incentive Management" software and find some of the big players. Just be warned they are not cheap and they often require significant reprogramming to work with the output from a TMS system. For smaller brokers, they often are not cost-effective. You can probably do just as well with a good Excel jockey (either on staff or outsourced).

The hardest part of ongoing administration is dealing with staffing changes—someone changes roles mid-year, new people are hired, others are fired, etc. Excel is a flat file, and tracking this kind of change requires a relational database. There are, however, many great minds out there in the transportation world, and I'm sure someone will put something out there soon to automate more complex incentive plans (beyond a flat percent-per-load). When they do, jump on it. The motivational value you will gain from having the details in front of your staff on a weekly or daily basis will be huge. But, in the meantime, you still need to make the effort to get them the information—even if it is in a very low-tech fashion. It's all good. Just as you don't need to go to an expensive gym to get fit—throw some bands over a door and do some curls—you'd be amazed what a little bit of effort and discipline with some very simple tools can do.

Appendix A

Does Incentive Compensation Really Work?

Lessons Learned from Using Incentive Compensation Design Principles on My Children

I have been designing incentive compensation plans for nearly my entire professional career. In that time, I've worked for massive organizations with thousands of employees and small start-ups with one or two employees. I've worked with banks, insurance companies, cement, faucet, and wiper-blade makers; professional services and food ingredient manufacturers; and of course, all manner of transportation and logistics companies. But some of my most significant lessons learned are from the times I experimented with incentives on my kids.

Lesson #1: Good News/Bad News

As I was starting my career with a global human resources consulting firm, I was also starting my family. I joined the big consulting firm two years after my first child (John) was born and learned the consulting business at the same time I was learning to be a mother. At age two, John developed a passion for Hot Wheels cars that lasted for many years, so when he started losing his teeth, his father and I decided that the tooth fairy should bring a Hot Wheels car instead of money. When he found the toy under his pillow the next morning, he was ecstatic; that was the absolute greatest thing ever! Lose a tooth and get a Hot Wheels car? (How many of you can see this one coming?)

The next night, after we had put him to bed, he came back out to the living room with blood streaming down his chin, proudly holding out two more teeth that he had bashed out by banging his face into the railing of his bed.

And thus, my first lesson learned in incentive design, and something we tell our clients to this day: *"The good news about incentives is they work. The bad news about incentives is they work."* So watch out for those unintended consequences.

Lesson #2: Always Define the Rules

About eight years later, when I thought I was getting pretty good at designing incentives, we developed a dandelion problem in our yard. I now had three children, ages ten, six, and three. As I contemplated the yard, and the pile of work I had to do, I thought to myself, "I have able-bodied children; they could do some of the work, and I can teach them some basic economic lessons and show them the value of hard work." So, I decided on a piece-rate incentive plan. I would pay them five cents for each dandelion they brought me, but it had to be the whole stem, not just the flower. Pleased with myself, I settled down to get a bit of work done. After a time, I realized they should have been finished: there couldn't have been that many dandelions in our yard. I looked outside but they were nowhere in sight. Our dandelions were also gone, though, so it had worked! When I called for them, they came running back to our yard, each with a small plastic grocery bag *full* of dandelions—from our yard *and* the three nearest neighbors' yards.

This was my second lesson: always think through the rules and boundaries of the incentive plan and outline them clearly for your workers. Consider as many of the ways they can (and will) interpret the rules in their favor, and lay out explicit guidelines about how gray areas will be handled. And always retain management discretion and gaming clauses in your plan documents. These clauses protect you when the unexpected happens and ensure you do not need to make payouts that are not financially commensurate with the business ROI. Needless to say, I leaned on my *own* management discretion clauses with my children that day.

Lesson #3: Clear Design Begets Clear Results

As my oldest child grew through elementary and junior high, he remained an average student. His standardized test scores were lackluster and in our school district, standardized tests determine placement in high school classes. In ninth grade, he was placed in only one honors class and it was recommended to us that he take a remedial study program. The notes on his standardized test results indicated that it was questionable whether he would be able to do college level work.

This was not my son. I knew he could do better, but I couldn't get him to care. He was smart, no doubt, and had figured out how to do just enough work to skate by. Nothing I did or said seemed to get him to realize how critical to his future his high school grades would be.

He finished sophomore year with B+s in all six classes. As I saw the chances of his having a shot at a college of his choice start to fade, I decided to crank up the motivation. We went on a mother/son summer road trip to visit six colleges and universities in Pennsylvania and New Jersey. I had hoped this would inspire him to buckle down and work harder.

It didn't.

Junior year started. I met with his guidance counselor, waived him into two honors classes, and added an optional seventh class to his schedule. John was less than thrilled, and his counselor gave us several stern warnings that if John couldn't handle the work, he could not drop back down to a lower-level class; his grades could be harmed even further. I swallowed hard and prayed that I had done the right thing.

He finished the first quarter with several incomplete or lost assignments and a weighted GPA of 3.29 (B+...again). And he got a C+ in German, which was the one class he had chosen entirely for himself. Something needed to be done.

At the FIATA conference in Los Angeles, a good friend and former client mentioned paying his child for each A. Why had I not done this before, particularly given what I do for a living? I think I was hoping John's intrinsic motivation would kick in. But it wasn't, and time was running out.

I thought for a bit about what I really wanted him to do, and it wasn't just a matter of getting more As. He needed to understand how bad grades hurt as much as good grades help, and that a B, given his current GPA, would have no effect. And those of you who have understood the lessons in this book are now smiling, as you can probably also see this coming.

I developed an incentive plan that had both an upside and a downside. It worked like this:

Table A.1: *Regular and Honors Class GPA Incentive Table*

Quarter Grade	Regular Class Value	Honors Class Value
C- (1.67)	-$250.00	-$187.50
C (2.00)	-$150.00	-$112.50
C+ (2.33)	-$50.00	-$37.50
B- (2.67)	-$25.00	-$18.75
B (3.00)	$0.00	$0.00
B+ (3.33)	$12.50	$25.00
A- (3.67)	$25.00	$50.00
A (4.00)	$75.00	$150.00
A+ (4.33)	$125.00	$250.00

Note: *Positive and negative values are illustrative. If you adapt this for your child, use values that you are comfortable paying out, yet big enough to get your child's attention.*

The idea was that he would lose more from a bad grade in a class like PE than he would from a bad grade in Honors Physics, but he could gain more from a good grade in Honors Physics than he could from a good grade in PE. But because Honors grades are weighted, a bad grade in one of these classes would cost more than a good grade in a regular class would reward him. Yes, I thought about this a lot, and tested many possible outcomes to get it *just right* before I presented it to him. This is a best-practice for any incentive plan.

I showed him the plan and suddenly I had his full attention. He did the math and realized that straight A+'s could net him $1,250 per quarter—that was $3,750 for the remainder of the year. I had gulped myself when I had modeled this out, but I had already assessed the risk of his ability to get straight A+'s (small) and then I looked at my upside: if he *did* pull off straight A+'s for the last three quarters he could get into a position to get enough scholarship money to save me far more than the $3,750; my ROI was just fine. We had a brief negotiation about discrete versus cumulative periods, as he was concerned that his poor performance in Q1 would drag his average down, so I decided to err on the side of motivational value and agreed to count each quarter separately rather than average them together.

It worked like a charm!

During second quarter midterm Parent-Teacher Conferences, every one of his teachers commented on his remarkable transformation: he was taking notes in class rather than falling asleep; he was paying attention to deadlines and asking for extra credit assignments.

He finished second quarter with a 3.83 GPA, a payout of $425, and a 98 percent on his German final. The third quarter ended with a 3.73 GPA, a payout of $400, and his first solid A in Honors Physics. In the last quarter, during which he also took two ACT exams, he finished with a 3.97 GPA and a payout of $525. With the $1,350 he had justly earned, he bought himself the seven-string guitar he'd been wanting and I saw his overall high school GPA raise from barely a 3.3 to just above 3.6, with a 17 percent improvement in his class rank.

For those of you who may be worried that this somehow damaged his intrinsic motivation, he was self-motivated for the ACT exams and finished with a score respectable enough for admission consideration at most colleges and for scholarship money at many. One of his scores is indicative of the change: on all prior pretests he'd never broken twenty on the reading portion, and yet he got a twenty-nine on the real thing, and I had offered and paid him *nothing* for the ACT results[22]. Instead, I simply took him out for a celebratory lunch after the scores came in. It seems that the cash incentive for his grades was the trigger that was needed to get his intrinsic motivation turned on. He learned that he could succeed if he tried, and that has spilled over into many other areas of his life.

At the time of this writing, John has completed the first half of his junior year at Valparaiso University in Indiana where he is completing a five-year International Engineering Program with a double major in Electrical Engineering and German and minors in Math and Physics. He has made Dean's List all semesters so far and has carried no less than seventeen credits per term. He also earned a significant scholarship, so the ROI on the incentive plan came to fruition.

---

[22] For those of you not familiar with the ACT, a 36 is a perfect score and anything higher than 25 or 26 is solid college material.

His younger sister, however, has provided yet another valuable lesson in the art and science of incentive compensation design. She is four years younger than John, so I thought it would be easy when she hit high school (been there, done that, you know?). Boy, was I wrong. I put her on John's incentive plan freshman year and...nothing. She couldn't care less. She struggled with the change in expectations that came along with being in high school and exhibited some of the same issues I saw with John: missing or late assignments, not doing extra credit work and not taking advantage of test-retakes to improve her grades. Like her brother had been, she was living in 3.0 land (and barely hanging onto that). So, I decided I needed to go back to the drawing board and figure out what would truly motivate her. I realized she needed a more immediate reward. Waiting ten weeks until the end of a quarter for the payout was too long. She needed weekly encouragement and it needed to be tied directly to the things she wasn't doing: extra credit and test retakes.

So, I developed a program wherein each week, I would look at what extra credit assignments or test retakes were completed and pay a dollar value for each one, paid out each Friday. I quickly realized a potential "unintended consequence" here, as she could fail tests to give herself more opportunities to get paid for retakes. Definitely not what I was looking for. I discussed this with her and she suggested that I include a payout for any test or quiz that she gets an A on (93 percent or better). I agreed and said. "I'll go one better—if you get 100 percent. I'll double the payout."

She completed the program the second half of sophomore year, and here are her grades.

Table A.2: *Extra Credit and Test Retake Compensation Plan Impact on Grades*

Course	Before New Plan				After New Plan			
	Q1	Q2	Exam 1	Sem 1	Q3	Q4	Exam 2	Sem 2
PE	A-	A-	C-	B+	A+	A	C-	A-
English*	B	B	B	B+	B	B+	B	B+
AP Psych*	B	B-	C-	B-	A-	A	A+	A
Chemistry	B+	A-	A-	A-	A	A	A-	A
Math	B	B-	B+	B	B-	C+	C-	B-
APUSH*	B	C+	C-	B-	A	B+	C+	B+
French	A-	B+	B	B+	B+	B	B+	B+
GPA	**3.34**	**3.14**	**2.65**	**3.24**	**3.68**	**3.53**	**2.94**	**3.58**

* represents an Honors or AP course.

Q3 was the first quarter she got above a 3.4 in high school, and she was texting me when she completed extra credit assignments and received a high score on a quiz or test. She asked every Friday for me to calculate her pay and really enjoyed getting the weekly cash influx (though it cost me a bit more than I expected!) Clearly we still need to work on her exam-taking strategies, though it's an interesting puzzle as she took the AP Psych and U.S. History exams as a sophomore and earned a 4 and a 3, respectively, so she knows how to do well on exams. I just don't have quite the right carrot out there yet for her to buckle down on regular exams. I will tackle that challenge next year.

While her brother was fine with a big payment at the end of the quarter, Katie needed a more immediate reward to see the benefit. Your employees will have similar differences in terms of what motivates them. While it's not practical to tailor the incentive plan to each employee, you can use a variety of the motivational techniques I've discussed in this book to try to cover as many bases as you can with one program. Use career levels, merit based salary increases, recognition and reward programs, and incentive elements that payout on different frequencies (some monthly, some quarterly) and you will capture the attention of more of your population.

I have one more to get through high school and this one is completely different than the other two (he refuses to let me pay for grades and yet in 7th grade he's already had a significant problem with turning in assignments late or not at all), so I'll be digging into those other motivational tools (recognition, probably, or maybe some kind of career-level progression or non-monetary reward scheme) very soon. I'll keep you posted.

Appendix B

About the Author

Beth Carroll is a transportation and logistics compensation expert. She is a thought leader on future trends in variable pay programs, truck driver pay, sales compensation, and using compensation to motivate employees. In her articles, speeches, and books she explains the psychology, mathematics, and industrial sociology of compensation. She is the owner of Prosperio Group, a consulting firm which helps companies maximize profitability by clarifying business objectives, rationalizing organization structures and roles, and driving performance through effective compensation. Beth has decades of experience developing incentive plans for multi-billion dollar global firms across all industries and has worked with more than one hundred transportation and logistics companies. Prosperio manages the Compensation Survey: MeasureUp, which covers many roles found throughout the transportation and logistics industry.

For more information about buying multiple copies of this book or if you would like to have Beth as a keynote or workshop presenter, please e-mail: beth.carroll@prosperiogroup.com.

Appendix C

Acknowledgments

I would like to first and foremost acknowledge the freight broker-owners and managers that I have worked with through the years who have both taught me and helped shape the ideas and stories that are found in these pages. I hope that you have learned as much from me as I have from all of you, and I hope to continue to give back to this industry for many years to come.

There are some specific people who come to mind as shining lights from my early years of trying to make it on my own, the first of whom is Mike Fouts, my first transportation client, who patiently explained what a backhaul was and who first suggested that my knowledge of compensation design might be of value to this industry. Next on the list would be Brian Evans, owner of L&L Freight. Not only did Brian give me the most glowing introduction possible during my second TIA appearance, but he has also been a true friend, confidant, and supporter throughout my years of learning and growing with this industry.

Other luminaries in this industry and guides during my early years include: Geoff Turner, Jeff and Jim Tucker, Keith Gibson (you are missed), Rob Gale, Pete Hill, Rob Robinson, Chad and Jeff Blakeman, Matt Meeks, Sarah Ruffcorn, Michael McKinney, James Kerr, Rick Barker, Michael Caney, Bob Voltmann, Cindy Amos, Joel McGinley, James Kenny, Charlie Saffro and so many others who will share a special place in my heart and mind for all that I have learned from them.

Of course, none of this would be if on a day in the early fall of 2007, my husband, John Carroll, had not said, "you could do this on your own, you know." He has supported me, peeled me off the ceiling more times than I can count, and has endured countless vacations spent sitting poolside with me and my computer and phone. My kids have also endured the travel that goes with this job, which while it enabled me to meet so many wonderful people and learn enough to be able to write this book, it also meant many missed performances, missed parent-teacher conferences, a few missed birthdays, and the necessity of mothering through colds and heartbreaks via text message and phone call. Thanks to you all for your support.

Also, tremendous thanks to Henry DeVries and Denise Montgomery at Indie Books, who gave me the information and support to take all the bits of writing that already existed and turn them into a book. Denise's editorial talent and patience in the face of technological difficulties is unmatched.

Appendix D

Index

Made in the USA
Coppell, TX
30 April 2022

77230869R00083